Henry A. Blake

Pictures from Ireland

Henry A. Blake

Pictures from Ireland

ISBN/EAN: 9783337322434

Printed in Europe, USA, Canada, Australia, Japan

Cover: Foto ©Andreas Hilbeck / pixelio.de

More available books at **www.hansebooks.com**

PICTURES FROM IRELAND

BY

TERENCE McGRATH

SIXTH EDITION

LONDON

KEGAN PAUL, TRENCH & CO., 1, PATERNOSTER SQUARE

1888

CONTENTS.

PICTURES FROM IRELAND.

CHAPTER I.

AN IRISH LANDLORD OF THE OLD SCHOOL.

To the Irish landlord the year 1879 will present itself in time to come as one of the saddest in his history. In 1848, when famine decimated the people, the bonds of sympathy still existed between them and their landlords. The movement of 1867 was purely "national," and its subsidence restored the friendly feeling that had hardly been interrupted. But the present agitation is different. Led by men who "dare do all that may become" an agitator, but who carefully abstain from the post of danger with the rabble maddened by their teaching, the tenants have themselves cut the cord of sympathy with the landlords, and turned upon them with a savage vituperation as undeserved as it was unexpected.

Mr. Kirkland lives on a property that has been

B

in the possession of his family for nearly 300 years. No blight of absenteeism has passed over the place, where the well-trimmed lawns and drives, and carefully tended timber, afford constant work to many labourers. With the inherited instincts of his class, he has a firm belief in the moral inferiority of the Roman Catholic people, yet in years gone by he has acted liberally towards his tenants, who are mainly Roman Catholic. No tenant has ever appealed to him in vain, his purse and his influence being equally at their service. He has even given a site for a new chapel and a subscription towards its erection. In ordinary times things have always gone smoothly enough; and the new agent who ten years ago suggested an increase of the rental, which he declared could be effected without hardship to the tenants, was answered so decidedly that he did not again allude to the subject. Feeling himself bound to stand by his tenants in any strait, and ready to do so against all comers, he has a firm belief that the bounden duty of his tenants is to stand by him, which he interprets by the entire subordination of their social and political ideas to his.

Thus every election before the change effected by the Ballot Act resulted in strained relations that took some time to settle. For weeks before the momentous day the agent or rent-warner was busy among the tenants. Leaseholders were asked to remember how long the family had lived on the estate. That cattle-shed about which there was some difficulty could be built, and timber and slates were readily promised. Tenants at will were more sternly reminded of that fact, and after former elections had learned how bitterly Mr. Kirkland could resent the adverse vote that he looked on as the basest ingratitude.

On the other hand, the popular side had generally a sturdy champion in the parish priest, who is considered by Mr. Kirkland, in his secret heart, as a dangerous viper to whom all the troubles of the country can be traced. Busy as the agent might be with the tenants, Father Pat was not a whit behind, either in the persuasiveness of his canvass or the rigour of his denunciation.

"What am I to do, Father Pat?" said the distraught Tom, who had been visited by the agent. "Sure I cannot see myself turned out on the roadside with my little family, like Will Delany afther the last election."

"Tom, you must be a true man and stand by your country and your Church."

"Troth, I would surely, if I dared; but your Riverince knows that I cannot go against the masther."

"Very well, Tom, be a renegade at your peril; but as you have deserted your clergy, so your Church will desert you in your hour of need."

Tom was triumphant at having escaped the danger of opposition to the landlord, and trusted to time to make his peace with the Church. But he miscalculated the power of Father Pat's resources. At home he found his wife in tears. The priest had been with her, and shown her how much better it were for her husband that he had a millstone tied about his neck and were flung into the sea than that he should be a renegade to his religion. His name would be execrated from the steps of the altar, and heaven would be closed against him. Manfully as he might resist, the parish priest was too strong for him. His neighbours looked askance at him. His wife was about to present him with another of those branches that grow so thickly on the Irish family tree ; and who could tell what the consequences might be? He did not quite believe in the power of Father Pat to endow the promised increase with horns like a goat, but his wife did ; and, so implicit was her faith and abject her terror, that he felt he must choose between his promise and her life. Of course he yielded. Probably, if he had any ideas on the subject at issue between the landlord and the priest they coincided with the views of the latter ; but neither his feelings nor the pressure to which he was subjected were accepted by Mr. Kirkland as an excuse for what he called an ingrained baseness, and he sighed with regret that Oliver Cromwell's life had not been prolonged for fifty years.

Sometimes the tenant stood by the landlord,

and, having been removed a week before the
election to a place where with other "faithful"
tenants he was safe from being kidnapped by his
neighbours, he was, on the day of the polling, sent
to the booth on cars escorted by dragoons or in-
fantry, and ran the gauntlet of jeering crowds who
lined the road and flung stones at him, or women
who on their knees cursed him with frightful im-
precations as a Judas and a renegade.

Now all this is changed by the Ballot Act, and Mr.
Kirkland has thrown up the sponge, leaving Father
Pat in full possession ; for what man can conceal
from the wife of his bosom how he has voted? and
what woman could hope to hide the knowledge
from a questioner so practised as the parish priest?
By removing these periodical strains, the ballot
has done something towards reducing the friction
between landlord and tenant to more legitimate
limits ; and on looking back at the worry, danger,
and expense of the open voting, even Mr. Kirkland
feels that he can contemplate a coming election
with an equanimity that partially repays him for
the loss of a power not always exercised with judi-
cious forbearance. Mr. Kirkland liked his tenants,
and when no disturbing element has cropped up he
has always been fairly popular with them, as in
money affairs he is generous. But in the matter of
insisting on the annual whitewashing of their houses,
and using a gate for the entrance to a field instead
of a gap stopped with an easily moved cartwheel or

spare plough, they consider him a trifle dictatorial. His rents remain as he found them on coming into possession thirty years ago and average the Government valuation, which is about 35 per cent. under the present fair letting-value; but he is astonished to find that neither are his tenants more comfortable nor are his rents better paid than on the adjoining property, bought in 1852 for a few years' purchase by a speculating attorney, who has raised his rents 50 per cent. and insists on their being paid up to the day.   His tenants' houses are outwardly cleaner, and their fences better made, but money in bank or elsewhere they have not.

An application has been made by one of them for permission to sell his interest to one of the rack-rented over the way; who has somehow not only contrived to pay the rent, but to lay by a little money, which he will gladly expend in the purchase of another small farm at the other side of his fence, the rent of which is not much more than half the rate at which he pays for his own land.   This exercises Mr. Kirkland much, who sometimes has a hazy idea that his tenants take things more easily than their neighbours, upon whom the necessity for making the increased rent has forced habits of industry not natural to the happy-go-lucky Celt.   Down to the passing of the Land Act Mr. Kirkland always supplied the timber and slates for any building undertaken by a tenant, whether leaseholder or otherwise;

but since the passing of that Act he has refused to continue the practice, except on condition that 5 per cent. on the cost of materials is added to the rent ; and the not unfrequent declaration by the tenants that they " don't see what use the Land Act is at all at all " is balm to his wounded feelings.

Hitherto Mr. Kirkland's life has been fairly worth living, though his neighbour, Mr. Cregan, the successful attorney, has been of late a thorn in his side. Mr. Cregan, having found himself the possessor of a property of some hundreds a year, determined, as soon as the depression following the famine had passed away, to make his purchase a paying speculation. He therefore announced a revaluation, and at a stroke increased his rental 15 per cent. But first he did a politic thing. Mr. Cregan was a Roman Catholic, and he built on his property a new house for the parish priest. This gave him a powerful friend, and the revaluation was acceded to with some grumbling. No person was more irate than Mr. Kirkland, who made no secret of his contempt for the latest addition to the landed gentry of the county, or his displeasure that the people should be oppressed by what he considered an unjustifiable rise of rent. Did he not find that a heavy percentage of his own rent was always unpaid ? And how could any people pay a larger rent for land to which his was not inferior ? However, somehow the rents were paid ; and when again and again Mr. Cregan raised his rents, the tenants still paid with a regularity that puzzled Mr. Kirkland not a little. But Mr. Cregan's revenge had come. With the first wave of the present agitation he saw that it appealed to passions too strong to be allayed without considerable difficulty. That the people had had two bad harvests could not be gainsaid, and yet his rents had been punctually paid. Now, when the demand was announced of a reduction of 25 per cent. or no rent, Mr. Cregan not alone gave a reduction to that amount on the half-year's rent due — the remainder of which was promptly paid—but was one of the fiercest denouncers of tyrants who refused to grant a similar concession. Bonfires blazed for him. Thousands cheered him when he appeared at the anti-rent meetings, and the tenants of other properties declared that, "Ould or new stock, he was the man for the people."

Mr. Kirkland's tenants ask for a similar reduction, but ask in vain. He says, "Your land is let to you 50 per cent. under the rent that Mr. Cregan has been charging. And even now your ordinary rent is 25 per cent. lower than the reduced amount paid by his tenants." The tenants have come in a body to his office to make their demand, and, being refused, have walked out without paying a penny. In vain he has told them that if they require time to pay their rent they shall have it, as it has always been given. No, they require no time. They cannot and they dare not pay if they do not get an abatement of 25 per cent., no matter what the land is let for. Next day the bailiff came in, and begged respectfully to resign his position.

"Why, Brady," Mr. Kirkland said, "you have been for twenty years a bailiff on the property, and I think you ought not now to leave me in a difficulty."

"Did your honour hear about last night?"

"No ; what is it?"

"Well, about five shots were fired in through my window, and the bed is riddled ; and only for the mercy of God and the thickness of the feather bed that rose up outside me, I would be a dead man."

"This is horrible, Brady. You must have police protection."

"Faith, I will not have police protection, your honour. I'll rise out of it entirely. Sure life is sweet."

"But your life cannot be in danger if you have police always with you."

"Sure your honour would not have me disgrace my little family by having police with me?"

"How can that disgrace you?"

"Would not it be a disgrace to have it said I was such a bad member that the police had to guard me? No, faith, I won't have anything more to do with it. Would it not be better for your honour to give the five shillings in the pound than to be fighting with the people?"

"No, Brady; I never will give it. I have always acted justly and fairly towards my tenants, and I will not now be dictated to by a lot of scoundrels who have not between them the value at stake of the platform they stand on."

"Well, master, for God's sake take care of yourself, for these are dangerous times; and I'll tell you the truth, the country is speaking hard about you, so don't put yourself in danger. I'll go now, your honour; and I am sorry to have to leave you."

Mr. Kirkland is now busily engaged in preparations for a prolonged residence abroad. His servants and labourers are all discharged, and he has appointed an agent with instructions to get the rent, or eject every tenant on the estate. No man touches his hat to him as he passes. Dark hints have been conveyed from various quarters that his life is not safe. Police patrols are never absent from the place; and he, who has all his life been a thorough Irishman, feeling a personal pride in every honour gained by a countryman, now hates the people with a reciprocity for which they were not prepared. He has learned a lesson from Mr. Cregan. With returning prosperity he will insist on the tenants paying the full value of his land; and if in future years the tenants determine that a temporary reduction is necessary, he can respond without feeling that his compliance is a weak surrender to an unjust demand.

CHAPTER II.

A LAND JOBBER.

WHEN, after the crisis of 1848, the grasp of the creditors tightened round the Newbroom Estate, the tenants joined heartily in the determination to prevent the service of documents from the Encumbered Estates Court, necessary as a preliminary to the sale of the property and the removal of a landlord between whom and the tenants no cloud had ever come. Many and crafty, and not always unsuccessful, were the plans of the wily bailiffs to effect "personal service;" and Colonel Brown gave up the active performance of his magisterial duties after that drunken prisoner, brought before him by two policemen, presented him unexpectedly with a paper, at the same time informing him that it was a correct copy of the original then and there exhibited. Nothing could save the property, which was sold in due course for about fifteen years' purchase, and the hearts of the tenants sank when they heard that their new landlord was Mr. Clancy.

Mr. Peter Clancy was not unknown to the people

of Newbroom. It was not many years since he worked upon his father's farm in the neighbourhood, and respectfully touched his hat to Colonel Brown whenever they met. But, the clever son of a clever and hard-working father, he soon took a farm for himself. Adding cattle-jobbing to his other pursuits, and taking farm after farm as they fell vacant after '46, he found himself the possessor of many flocks and herds. When the land panic followed the famine, he was not slow to see the facility with which property could be acquired; and his first venture returned him at the existing rental over 11 per cent. To purchase that he had sold his stock and disposed of his farms; and the property gave him a nucleus by mortgaging which he was enabled to continue his purchases.

Mr. Peter Clancy, J.P., has now been for twenty-seven years the owner of Castle Clancy—for so Newbroom has been rechristened, with the Irish love of high-sounding names. In that time he had bought and sold more than double that number of properties, and his enemies are to be counted by the number of people who from time to time have been his tenants. The Narrowmore property, with a rental of £2000 a year, was purchased by him for £32,000. In four years a rearrangement of the rental had been made. The tenants complained loudly. They were reminded that Mr. Clancy was a practical farmer who knew well the real value of the land. They refused to pay. Mr.

Clancy was quite willing to take up the land, and in due course evicted four or five tenants whose farms joined, and placed his own stock upon them. His cattle were killed. He swore informations and recovered the amount, which was levied off the tenants. Ultimately, having inundated him with threatening letters, they gave in, and agreed to the increased rental. Sympathy with the tenants Mr. Clancy never affected, nor did he acknowledge any duties towards them. "You want to live out of a farm, and you pay me the value. You owe me nothing but the rent ; I owe you nothing but the receipt." This has been his creed, and he has always refused to go one step beyond it. Cursed from many an altar in many a county, he has held on the principles thus adopted, and in five years he resold the Narrowmore Estate for £60,000, having raised the rental to £3000 per annum.

The history of the Narrowmore property is that of every estate that has passed through his hands. Properties have been purchased by him, subdivided into plots so small that the tenants must of necessity be paupers. To tenants of that stamp America was open, and to America they must go. With indomitable determination he cleared them off, and resold a property "pulled together" and revalued, leaving to the new purchaser a number of tenants better in condition than before, but hating the name of landlord, and loathing the man who would not let them follow the same system of subdivision that their fathers followed before them.   With the tenants on what he intended to retain as the family estate, Mr. Clancy has been a little more cautious, but he now regrets that he has settled in the country in which he was known; for even if he were generous as he is grasping, he can never hope to taste the sweets of social position in the neighbourhood where he knows that by the tenants he is hated, and has an uncomfortable suspicion that by the gentry he is despised.

Nor in truth is it to be wondered at, for Mr. Clancy is not quite straight in his dealings.   Loud in his professions of stern integrity, his bond is much more acceptable than his word, and his performance of magisterial duties is not above suspicion.   For Mr. Clancy is a magistrate; has even been called on the grand-jury.   In the days gone by, before fortune had favoured him, he looked upon the commission of the peace as a social guarantee, and the appearance of a name on the grand-jury list is an " open sesame " to every house in the county.   So did his wife, worthy woman; and so did his daughters three; but in their hands the coveted honours have turned to Dead Sea fruit.   The gentlemen of the county will have none of him.   His only guests are the parish priest and the dispensary doctor; and old farmers who knew him before he had set up the carriage, with servants in ill-made liveries, have a

way of calling him "Peter" that is to him gall
and wormwood : for Mr. Clancy dislikes his countryman's weakness of yielding respect rather to good
birth than to prosperity. In politics he declares
himself a strong Liberal, with a dash of Nationalism,
though the latter is modified, as not being quite
genteel—that is, he will go with the parish priest
in anything not affecting the rights of property.
The Irish Church Act was satisfactory to him.
He is prepared to support any education bill advocated by Father Carey, and Home Rule would
give the whip hand to Roman Catholics of property. But there he stops. "Property has its
rights" is the axiom by which he holds, and in
all matters affecting the security of the landlords'
position he is a Tory of the Tories. The Land
Act has cost him thousands of pounds, and he
inveighs against it as subversive of all principles
of security.

Previously he had boldly declared the amount
of increase he considered the tenants should pay,
and offered eviction as the alternative ; but after
the passing of that Act some tenants chose the
latter, and claimed compensation, which was
granted by the chairman of the quarter sessions
to such an amount as seriously interfered with Mr.
Clancy's plans and profits. Still from time to
time as opportunity offered he has increased the
rent, now of this farm, now of that ; but never so
much at one time as would drive the tenant to

prefer eviction with the chance of compensation; for once settled in a farm, an Irish tenant will bear much rather than give up the homestead where he has lived for any time. The Castle Clancy Estate now pays 50 per cent. more than when the easy-going Colonel Brown went to the wall.

This agitation affects Mr. Clancy vitally. Owner of several properties, his income is derived from the margin over the interest on mortgages, and on some of his purchases interest or margin there is none. At the meeting held within a mile of Castle Clancy his name was mentioned amid the execrations of hundreds, who groaned as they marched passed the Gate-house, carrying banners, on which the mottoes, "Down with the land robbers," "Death to the tyrants," "Remember '48," are accepted by him as personal threats. To give Mr. Clancy his due, he is not frightened; were he a coward he had never dared to build a fortune on the outraged prejudices of a revengeful people. The non-payment of his rents for a single year would mean ruin, and the rent or the land he is determined to have. He has rather posed as fighting the battle of the landlords, and accuses his neighbour, Mr. Butler, of pandering to the vices of the rabble because at a magistrates' meeting the latter declared that if any man had raised his rents he ought now to give a substantial reduction.

Mr. Clancy's Castle Clancy tenants have attended the office, where they come determined to pay no rent without receiving a reduction of 30 per cent. Five or six armed policemen are walking about outside, and an inquisitive tenant may see the handle of a revolver in a convenient position on a ledge under the off-side of the desk at which the landlord sits. Mr. Clancy is not prepossessing in appearance. A low, retreating forehead, shaggy grey eyebrows, and deep-set cold blue eyes, are balanced by an ill-cut but broad and powerful nose, square massive chin, and the large mouth with retracted lips exposing the gums, so common among the Irish peasants.

"Well, boys; I hope you come to pay the rent like honest men," is Mr. Clancy's greeting, as the tenants file into the office one by one until the room is nearly full.

All eyes turn on John Heffernan, who is evidently the spokesman of the tenants. He clears his throat, and answers—

"Well, you see, Mr. Clancy, these are very hard times entirely."

"I don't see that at all, John. Except the loss on the potatoes, there is nothing to complain of."

"The Lord save us, sir! How can you say that? Isn't the turf as wet as dung on us? and aren't the cattle down to nothing? and don't you know well that there is no return in the oats at all? And, sure, there's no use talking of the potatoes; we could not get as much out of an acre as would feed the pigs."

C

"Go and tell that to Mr. Butler or to Lord Noodleton, John Heffernan; it won't do for me. I know exactly what you have and what it is worth. Go out to the yard, and you will see my turf that was cut by alongside yours. How comes it that my turf is dry if yours is wet? Have you dug your potatoes yet?"

"Troth, I have not. How could I get time?"

"Why, you have had fine weather for three months; but I suppose you did not like to dig them until they got frost-bitten. You say they are worth nothing?"

"Bedad, the acre that I have is not worth a pound."

"Very well; I will give you four pounds for the acre. So you can deduct that from your rent, and the potatoes are mine."

"There's no use beating about the bush, Mr. Clancy; we cannot pay our rent unless we get the reduction."

A loud murmur of assent runs round the room.

"I will give no reduction," Mr. Clancy says determinedly. "You have all taken your land and undertaken to pay the rent, and I must have either the rent or the land."

"Well, now, sir, the truth must be spoken. Don't you know that the rent is too high? Sure it's twice the valuation, and no person could pay that rent in times like these. Besides, you gave us a rise of rent in 1855 and again in '64 and again in '72, and we think now that you ought to give the reduction as well as every one else."

"I cannot listen to you. I must pay my debts, and you must pay yours."

"Sure, I would pay if I could," exclaims the Widow Henahan; "but you know that you doubled the rent on me since the first rise."

"Well, why did you not give up the farm if you thought it too dear?"

"Arrah, Mr. Clancy, how could I give up my little farm with my children growing up about me? What could I do? Sure, if you said I was to pay twice as much more I must strive to pay it or go into the poorhouse, and all I ask now is just to get the abatement."

"Yes," all exclaim; "all we want is the abatement; you rose the rent on us when the times were good, and we want you to give us justice now that the bad year has come."

"Does not every one know, your honour, that the land is not worth more than the valuation?" resumed John Heffernan.

The word valuation arouses the ire of Mr. Clancy. "Valuation!" he shouts. "Don't talk to me of the valuation. Do you know the Government valuation was three-quarters of the real value of land in 1852, when the market prices were—I'll tell you what they were per hundredweight: Wheat, 7s. 6d.; oats, 4s. 10d.; barley, 5s. 6d.; butter, 65s. 4d.; beef, 35s. 6d.; mutton, 41s.; pork, 32s.? Do you know that the average value of these things for the last four years is 45 per cent. greater than when the land was valued? And you complain of an increased rent!"

"We do, sir; we don't know much about what you are talking of; but the rent is more than doubled on some of us; and we think, and Father Greaney thinks, we ought to get the reduction."

"All right; you owe me a year's rent, and I will eject every one of you. I was prepared for this," Mr. Clancy says, as his bailiff, who has been standing at the door of the office, hands an ejectment process to the first man who turns to leave. This is a fatal blow. Ready as are the tenants to resist within certain limits, and to trust to the chapter of accidents during the months, possibly, before the processes could be served, they feel that here they are in a trap, and know that Mr. Clancy will carry out his threat of having the land or the rent.

Once get the better of an Irishman, and for the time he is cowed utterly; so John Heffernan turns sullenly and without a word produces the full amount of his rent, for which he receives a receipt duly. One after another every one has paid; and while they wend their way homeward, bitterly and fiercely cursing the man whom they acknowledge their master in cunning as he is in determination, Mr. Clancy sits writing a letter to a friend, in which he says :—" This agitation is certainly most dangerous, and some people have had a great deal of trouble; but I must say that my Castle Clancy tenants came in and paid up the full amount without a murmur."

CHAPTER III.

AN ABSENTEE'S AGENT.

IRISH agents, like Irish potatoes, pigs, and patriots, are separable into two broad divisions—the good and bad, and among the former Mr. Brereton may fairly be classed. The house of Knockraymond is one in which even the lordly income of its owner might be worthily spent, and Mr. Brereton, whose numerous family does not occupy more than a small portion of it, regrets that its owner has never seen its beauties or its capabilities. To the casual observer Mr. Brereton would appear to be the practical owner of the Knockraymond estate; but none know better than the tenants how little real assistance in time of trouble can be given by one who has himself no money to spare, and who openly declares that in his dealings between his employer and the tenant he must be just before he is generous. Mr. Brereton's ideas of an agent's duties are clearly defined: first, to secure the rent; secondly, to manage the property fairly, in the direction indicated by the owner; thirdly, to assist the tenants to the best of his ability; and fourthly, to take upon himself all the risks inseparable from the management of Irish properties. These duties he has faithfully performed for many years, yet he feels that the majority of the tenants fail to reciprocate his friendly feelings. On the Knockraymond estate he has striven to increase the size of the farms; and, as from time to time a small holding fell vacant without any immediate successor, he has refused another tenant, and divided the plot among adjoining holders. For this he has been denounced from the altar of the chapel hard by the gate as an exterminator who had quenched the fire of a homestead and assisted towards the destruction of a virtuous tenantry; and not even from the tenants between whom the holdings were shared did he receive any open expression of sympathy, or hear any deprecation of the crime, when that bullet whistled so unpleasantly close to his ear as he strolled one evening by some laurels near the house.

Long years ago, when Knockraymond House was built, the neighbouring town was stimulated by the presence of its owner; and, so far as Mr. Brereton considers himself justified in assisting, he is glad to contribute towards the maintenance of the modest public buildings. But he sees and regrets that the little town is gradually becoming more slipshod in appearance. The once busy hotel has become a public-house pure and simple.

The shops show dingy fronts, and the only new development is the branch bank that has opened in what was once the agent's house. There are many wants about the little town that only require an owner's eye to be supplied. That dilapidated footpath is sadly in need of repair, and a proper sewage system would be of undoubted benefit. Mr. Brereton has more than once mentioned these matters to the landlord, who replies that the people ought to learn how to help themselves, and instances the self-reliance and progression of the English village near which he resides; forgetting how materially it has benefited by the circulation of thousands of pounds drawn from Knockraymond. The agent's ideas of loyalty to his employer prevent his giving the answer in all its naked candour, and he has to bear the odium of refusing to comply with what the tenants consider a reasonable demand for assistance.

Mr. Brereton cannot remember the time when things went quite smoothly on the Knockraymond estate, and yet no man ever undertook an office with more anxiety to win the esteem of the people among whom he looked forward to spending the greater portion of his life. Determined to improve if possible the condition of the tenants, he began by changing the houses of an entire village from a swampy site beside a river to the opposite bank, where he flattered himself that he had earned the gratitude of the villagers by placing them on well-

drained ground and giving them holdings of more
than twice the value of their worn-out patches. He
forgot that the stream divided two parishes; and
from that moment he has experienced the sleepless
hatred of the parish priest, who has thus been
deprived of a portion of his flock and of his dues.
It certainly was hard upon the priest, whose income
was not so large that he could see with indifference
a whole village as effectually taken from him as if
its inhabitants had emigrated to America, and he
could not see why parochial arrangements of long
standing should be disturbed by an intruder. Nor
did the tenants to whom the new farms were
allotted, with assistance given in building better
houses, display the gratitude that was to be expected; and more than one of them saw with
unfeigned regret the destruction of the mud cabin
in which he was born. When Paddy Bane was
evicted, having fallen five years into arrear, Father
Dempsey attended at the head of a considerable
crowd, which he harangued, calling God to witness
the tyranny that had driven a respectable man,
with a helpless family, some of them lying on a
bed of sickness, to die on the roadside or languish
in the dismal wards of a workhouse. It mattered
not that the crowd knew Bane's shortcomings in
the matter of rent, and that his family was well
grown and in rude health. Such is the magic of
eloquence that they accepted the priest's statement
against the evidence of their senses; and for

months afterwards Mr. Brereton's safety was a matter of great anxiety to the police, the constable declaring that "he feared he had a bad chance of not being shot." Then, again, the prevention of the subdivision of Widow Flanagan's farm of eight acres into two holdings, one for each son, was the theme of more than one discourse from the altar steps of Knockraymond Chapel. "What do we want?" exclaims Father Dempsey. "Population —the bone and sinew of a country—the true source of a nation's wealth; and yet this descendant of a Saxon turns Michael Flanagan, a respectable man, adrift upon the wide inhospitable world. Know ye not the words of the poet—

> 'But a bold peasantry, their country's pride,
> When once destroyed, can never be supplied?'

Are ye men, that this thing can be? or slaves that a tyrant may exterminate, in the hope that bullocks may replace you?" The groans that greet Mrs. Brereton as she drives past the congregation on her way from church supply the answer, and add to the nervousness become chronic since her husband had the good luck to receive the agency of Knockraymond. Mr. and Mrs. Brereton alternate between three mental states—quiescence, uneasiness, and alarm. The blessing of peace is not often felt. In the second state the family is particular about loitering at windows in the evening. In the third, a state of siege is proclaimed. Outdoor business is

done as much as possible in the middle of the day.
Dining out is given up ; and altogether a state of
mind is engendered that looks upon every man as
a possible hero anxious to rid the world of a tyrant.
Mr. Brereton has become accustomed to it ; but the
careworn face and the silvered hair tell another tale
for Mrs. Brereton—her experience being rather
that of the performing sheep which thrusts its head
nightly into the lion's mouth, but generally dies
early of heart disease.

Mr. Brereton has long given up answering the
attacks made upon him. Letters are written in the
local papers containing lies so glaring that his
friends laugh at them ; but they all go to keep the
spark aglow that, right or wrong, is always kept
burning. The most circumstantial account has
been given of the death, from fever, of Bane's child.
The removal of Michael Flanagan has been called
a cold-blooded eviction ; "all several sins, all used
in each degree," have been laid at his door by
various correspondents, of whom the clergy are
sometimes not ashamed to sign their names. And
yet the tenants in their calmer moments acknowledge that he is a just man, and true to his word.
Year after year he has advanced tons of meal to
tenants at his own risk, the tenants paying for it
when the harvest is gathered. They do not thank
him, and believe the advance is made by order of
the landlord. And even though Mr. Brereton has
refused the bribes once freely offered, they cannot

understand that a man whose interest in the property is transient can trouble himself about the
welfare of tenants with whom at any moment his
connection may be severed.

Mr. Brereton's position has been made more
difficult by his being also agent to the Ballynolan
property.   Here £4000 a year is collected from
twelve hundred tenants, whose "farms" average the
valuation of £3 per annum.   From the first moment
he has given up any idea of improvement here as
hopeless.   Subdivision has gone so far that even
Irish ingenuity in making landed provision for
swarms of children is at fault.   The property bears
the relation to Knockraymond that a tramp's
kitchen does to an hotel ; and the crowds of cabins,
with their loads of rotten thatch surmounting dank
green walls, are regarded by the owners as an
Indian looks upon his wigwam—a place to hold the
women and children while he is away on his hunting grounds.   The Ballynolan tenant leaves annually
his dirty but healthy brood while he migrates to
England, where, as a harvester, he earns the amount
of his rent, and enough besides to supplement with
meal the produce of the potato plot tilled by his
wife and children in his absence.   When the model
farms were advocated as one of the panaceas for
Ireland's backwardness, Mr. Brereton pointed to
Ballynolan as an answer.   Here every tenant sees
year by year the best system of farming.   He works
early and late, assists in the clearance of weeds,

and must observe the result of care and neatness. His plot at home is so small that it could be kept like a garden. Yet on his return from England he rises at nine o'clock, lounges idly all day round his reeking cabin, leaving his wife to dig the half-tilled and ill-grown potatoes for dinner ; after which he visits his neighbours' houses, playing cards or listening to exciting discourses in his native tongue on the approach of England's downfall and Ireland's freedom until night, when he flings himself with his wife and family, men, women, and children, into a common bed. From this property Mr. Brereton must collect the rents as best he can, the bailiff generally watching the return from England, when the rent may be paid before the money has been spent. A whisper that emigration would be assisted was received as a challenge to the death, and among the five or six thousand souls who swarm on Bally-nolan are many who in entertaining the idea of shooting an agent would only consider *per contra* the remote possibility of detection. So Mr. Brere-ton has let them be.

Not that he has made no friends. He has found among the tenants men as honest as he could desire ; men, too, who understand his difficulties and appreciate his efforts to improve their position by increasing their farms to good workable size ; and if they have not spoken openly in his favour when attacks have been made upon him, Mr. Brereton in turn recognizes the difficulty and danger of an adverse outspoken opinion by men of their class.   But when after the Flanagan affair, Thady Ryan had agreed to shoot him for a consideration, timely information was given to him of every phase in the conspiracy, and he had the consolation of feeling that among the tenants he was not without friends, even though their practical friendship only carried them so far as to act as spies from the enemies' camp.   These men have declared to him in confidence that they disapprove of the meetings, from which they have not the courage to absent themselves.   Since the crusade against landlords they have come to the house by stealth and paid their rents, requesting Mr. Brereton to keep the receipts lest by any chance such damning evidence of integrity might be found in their houses.   Among the Ballynolan tenants, too, are many with whom Mr. Brereton has retained amicable relations.   Here the rent has always been dependent upon the proceeds of the English harvesting trip.   When sickness fell upon the head of a family the rent has been allowed to run into arrear, and ultimately written off or compounded for a small proportion of the whole debt ; and the average shortcomings always enter into the calculation of the income.   No tenant has ever been evicted, for save by wholesale emigration there could be no hope of improving the property ; and the advantage in any given case is so small as not to be worth the risk of an eviction.   That risk is as a rule in inverse ratio to the size of a farm ; and few care to risk their lives for a principle where eight or nine pounds, representing three years' arrears, is the sum at stake.

The owner of Ballynolan would hail with delight any measure enabling him to sell the property to the State, and this year has wearied the agent with requests to lodge money that cannot be collected. He declares that if the tenants are not compelled to pay now they will equally refuse next year ; but Mr. Brereton, who knows that the money has not been earned in England, and knows, too, how unstable are the people and how unsuited for lengthened combination, advises that matters this year be not pushed to extremities, and promises that a good harvest will go far to obliterate the effects of this agitation. In that case the most violent will fall back into the old lines, until the approach of another election once more lets loose the " politicians " who are now so cleverly dipping into Anglo-Saxon pockets on both sides of the Atlantic.

CHAPTER IV.

THE TENANTS' FRIEND.

IF you tell Mr. Casey he is a blood-sucker, he will
not call you out, but if human ingenuity can com-
pass a mischief to you he will do it. And yet no
term in the English language could more clearly
describe him. From the moment when, as an
attorney's apprentice, he did surreptitious jobs by
drawing memorials for the victims of petty-sessional
justice, charging to the ignorant peasants even more
than his master could have extracted, to the time
when, as John Casey, Esq., Justice of the Peace, he
dazzled the town of Kilnamuck with an eruption
of crests on harness, carriage, traps, buttons, and
paper, he has never lost an opportunity of taking
every penny that could be screwed from any person
with whom he has had business relations. Mr.
Casey is a small squat figure with a broad fat face,
on which a beard has never grown, and a clammy
hand, the most hearty grasp of which is feeble.
He always meets you as if it was an unexpected,
a startling pleasure. If you met him on a prairie

he would look as if he had just run against you
round a corner.   It is many years since Mr. Casey
began life in Kilnamuck ; and from the time when
he pleaded infancy in defence of a process for the
price of a watch that had been sold to him on
credit, his master predicted that he would make his
mark.   Keen and patient, he worked hard and
watched his opportunities.   Nothing was too high
for him to snatch at, too low to grovel for ; and
from the moment when a payment of £9 4s. admitted him upon the roll of attorneys-at-law he
became the leader in the petty-sessions practice of
Kilnamuck and its neighbourhood, and soon monopolized the best cases at quarter sessions.   But well
as he understood the business of an attorney the
profession had no charms for him.   Before many
years he had for a client a man whose small property was deeply mortgaged.   It was not difficult
to persuade the owner that he had better live
abroad and leave to him the management of the
estate ; and from that moment his line was taken.
Mr. Casey took up his residence in Camlin House,
and paid regularly a small sum to the owner.   He
had taken a lease of the place, and, at a time when
labour was abundant, added to the house and re-
modelled the grounds.   The tenants had paid large
sums from time to time for various legal expenses
that they did not quite understand ; yet when the
owner of Camlin took it into his head to return, he
was presented with so enormous a bill of costs, and

such an amount charged for buildings and improvements, that ultimately he agreed to hand over the property to his agent and tenant for about five years' purchase and a receipt in full of all claims upon him. But Mr. Casey is a clever man ; and from time to time other small agencies were offered to him until the deeds and accounts of most of the property about him were in his office. It seemed absurd that Mr. Cornwall, whose income was only about five hundred a year, should have handed over the collection of his rents to Mr. Casey. But there are many troubles incidental to the collection of even five hundred a year ; and Mr. Casey managed somehow or other to get in the rents more freely than other people. But the Ballybotherem estate ! Twenty thousand a year let to small tenants, and an owner caring for nothing but the punctual transmission of rent, was a prize in agencies worth working for. Mr. Casey's nerves tingled with excitement as he thought of the perquisites, donations, and delicately arranged bribes that might be extracted from such a property, and his breath came short as he contemplated the social dignity that would accompany the appointment. The agent was on his death-bed, but Mr. Casey knew that a premature application to Mr. Melville would probably be fatal to his hopes. However, he and the doctor understood each other, and the earliest intimation was given of the agent's death. Fast as rail and steamer could take them, Mr. Casey and two of the principal tenants on the property went to France, where Mr. Melville was then living ; and the latter yielded to the prayer of the self-constituted deputation from the tenantry for the appointment of Mr. Casey as agent. This has been his El Dorado and haven of rest. In Ireland it is customary to appoint to the commission of the peace the agent of a large property, especially if the owner be an absentee. He is also called on the grand jury ; and, as far as county matters are concerned, is accepted in every sense as the representative of the property. Mr. Casey was obliged to take his name off the roll of attorneys before he could receive the commission of the peace. However, the law agent and solicitor for the various properties now under his charge is the man who had been his partner for so many years, and it is whispered that profits are still divided.

Mr. Casey's system is not simple. He sternly sets his face against any increase of rent, and from his seat at the board of guardians inveighs bitterly against eviction for whatever cause :—" I am the agent of several properties, and I humbly thank the Almighty that I have never yet sent a family houseless on the world. No, gentlemen ; in Europe there could not be found people more anxious to pay their rent; and I have always found that with a little kindness and patient indulgence the tenants of this country will always pay to the last farthing." Speeches like this are of frequent occurrence, and

Mr. Casey is accepted as the tenants' friend. He is most indulgent to the tenants in many ways; yet if they could count up the items it would startle them to see the amount of money over and above the rents that has found its way to the office. So far as fences are concerned, they may manage their own affairs as pleases them best, and if provision is to be made for a second son by a subdivision of the farm, Mr. Casey is always ready to oblige a tenant—for a consideration.

The fine old customs are kept up on these properties. In the old leases were often specified the number of "duty fowl"—*i.e.* fat turkeys or fat hens and chickens that were to be annually supplied to "the great house," and Mrs. Casey has no hesitation in accepting fat fowl from the tenants. Then it is only a mark of esteem that the tenants should send their carts and horses, and sow and gather the crops of an agent who speaks so beautifully about the people. If any one has declined, somehow he thinks better of it next year, and all goes on swimmingly. Mrs. Casey has another valuable perquisite, which in the good old times was always due to the landlord's wife. "Seal-money" meant the present given by the tenant on the completion and sealing of his lease. With Mrs. Casey it is interpreted very freely as the price of her favour; and the tenants know that the only chance of getting that agreement signed or having a share of that vacant farm is to obtain her interest. The pair of gloves with the fingers stuffed with bright golden sovereigns was only a delicate compliment paid by William Rooney for her kindness in speaking for him when he proposed for the farm at Tubbernacreega.

With the exception of some few unpleasant incidents Mr. Casey has had on the whole a successful time as agent. Mr. Melville's property is let much below its value, and the difficulty of his life is to conceal that fact from the owner. Low letting means a large margin for the indirect taxation that an Irish tenant is always ready to pay; and if a man can afford to give fifty pounds to Mrs. Casey and two hundred pounds to the outgoing yearly tenant for succession to a farm of twenty acres at the rent of £20 a year, it is manifestly more comfortable for the agent and the outgoing tenant than if the rent of the farm were raised to £25 and a smaller margin left for "tenant-right."

James Freney has never been forgiven for his treachery with reference to the farm of Loughnakerriga. Mrs. Casey had given her interest to Michael Hession, who had proposed for it at 25s. an acre; but Freney had some of that energy so hateful to Mr. Casey. Knowing how the wind blew, he went straight over to France and saw Mr. Melville; produced a deposit receipt for £500; offered 30s. an acre for the farm; and returned with a letter to Mr. Casey saying it was Mr. Melville's wish that Freney's offer be accepted.

Freney has lived to rue the day. Rumours have

been set on foot that his high offer has led Mr.
Melville to the conclusion that the property has
been underlet, and a revaluation may be looked for.
Freney has been denounced from the altar ; insulted
in the market-place ; abused by the Tenants' Defence Association, and treated generally as a traitor
to the tenants and his country. His rent must be
paid to the day, and for the trespasses committed by
the cattle of adjoining tenants he has no redress.
As well might a Turkish Christian appeal to the
authorities against a Mussulman as Freney attempt
to summon one of his neighbours. The amount
of little injuries done to him is extraordinary, and
he wishes heartily that he had left the farm to
Hession, and taken his chance for another in the
usual course.

Many threatening letters in connection with that
farm have been forwarded by Mr. Casey to Mr.
Melville. Of these letters the police have never
been told, nor has any hint been given to others of
their receipt. They form part of a series transmitted to Mr. Melville from time to time, effectually
staving off that promised or threatened visit to
his Irish property. To Mr. Casey Mr. Melville
feels that he owes a debt of gratitude for having
retained an agency fraught with danger, and that
gentleman has no idea of allowing so satisfactory
a feeling to subside.

Not that Mr. Melville would be quite safe if
he did come over, for, good man as is Mr. Casey,

the tenants are not well off. Their rents are low,
but they find somehow that they cannot well pay.
Then, every man has some pet grievance which
Mr. Casey knows how to put aside; but if the
landlord were to come he must listen, and possibly
decide between two determined disputants, and,
except when the landlord's character for unswerving
fair play has been established, an adverse decision
not unfrequently leads to awkward results. These
matters are rarely touched by Mr. Casey. He has
not forgotten the six months' trouble that followed
his arbitration on the dispute about Peter O'Donnell's
right of way. Indeed, it was not without misgiving
that O'Donnell agreed to his arbitration, for though
he had been going over that passage across Mick
Shea's farm to the bog for thirty years, he knew
that £15 of Shea's money had been transferred
to Mr. Casey when the former was allowed to
purchase the good-will of Paddy Burke's farm.
He was therefore not quite unprepared for the
decision that he must not use the passage again,
but must make a passage for himself. But Peter
O'Donnell was not the man to have patience
under what he considered an injury. For days
he was seen each morning standing opposite Mr.
Casey's door, and he left no argument unused
to induce the reversal of the decision. Then a
threatening notice was posted on Shea's gate that
if he closed the passage he might prepare his
coffin. Then Mr. Casey received a letter, saying

that he was a tyrant and had better prepare for his doom; and at length private information was given him that he must be very careful, for O'Donnell was determined to shoot him or to have him shot. Ultimately the matter was arranged by Mr. Casey requesting Shea to allow O'Donnell to use the passage as a favour. But now arbitrations are only undertaken in conjunction with Father M'Carthy, between whom and the agent most cordial relations exist.

Never did Mr. Casey more heartily congratulate himself on his foresight than when Michael Hession came to him in fear and trembling to warn him about O'Donnell. When Hession applied for Loughnakerriga farm he produced a deposit receipt as evidence of his solvency. "Bless my soul, Michael," he said, "you are worse than a fool to leave your money in the National Bank, receiving but six pounds a year for four hundred pounds. I cannot bear to see you robbed in that way; and I'll tell you what I can do for you. I will take the money myself and you shall have twelve pounds a year for interest. There, don't thank me. I am, perhaps, foolish in that way; but I do like to see the tenants treated fairly." The farm was still in the balance, and Michael handed over the deposit receipt. From that moment Michael Hession has felt the keenest interest in Mr. Casey's welfare, and that feeling is shared by many of the tenants who had money to lend. It stood Mr.

Casey in good stead in the O'Donnell affair, and
is a lasting insurance that, should unfortunately
any exposure be threatened with reference to his
indirect income from the property, he may count
upon the support of a number of the most prosperous of the tenantry. When, with great difficulty, the loan was obtained for the owner of
Camlin at 7 per cent., that gentleman did not
suspect that a considerable portion of the sum was
the money lent to the agent by his own tenants
at 3 per cent.

It would be a gross exaggeration to say that
Mr. Casey is disliked by the people. Honest they
know he is not, and Paddy Malley cannot help
cursing his name when he remembers how, because
William Dwyer had two horses to lend, he got the
contract for the few perches of road that ran through
Malley's land. Still, he is full of the gambling
spirit, and hopes that perhaps next year before
the road sessions, when his wife will have presented
a couple of fat turkeys to Mrs. Casey, he may
secure Mr. Casey's interest for another job.

For at road sessions Mr. Casey is most useful.
John Greany wants a fence to his land, and a contract to make it at the expense of the barony would
be worth £20 to him, as he could use his horses
in the idle season. Father M'Carthy has arranged
the matter with Mr. Casey, who has passed it at
road sessions, the constitution of which seems
specially framed to throw the business into the

hands of a few anxious jobbers. When the matter
of Greany's fence came before the grand jury it
was hotly opposed. The fence was not required,
and the jury did not see their way to confirming
the presentment; but Mr. Casey made a long
speech, in which he warned the grand jury of
the impropriety of a non-elective body refusing
a presentment passed by the ratepayers. The
jury yielded. Father M'Carthy was not the worse
at Easter for that £20 paid to Greany, and
Mr. Casey bore out his character for helping a
friend. With the grand jury he is unpopular, as
he has a way of posing as the champion of an
oppressed people, and appealing to the grand jury
to do something in their interests that had already
been decided upon.

Mr. Casey has hopes that in due time Mr.
Melville will sell the Ballybotherem property, when
he is prepared to come forward with an offer.
What more probable than that Mr. Melville would
take sixteen or seventeen years' purchase of a
property on which, by the urgent advice of his
agent, he has remitted 30 per cent. this year, and
about the future prospects of which he receives
the most gloomy account? In the mean time, Mr.
Casey has no objection to the introduction of a
large measure for the creation of a small class
of peasant proprietors. The smaller the better,
for Mr. Casey knows how few years will roll past
before the re-sale of such small properties must

begin. And he has hopes. His ideal tenant is a man holding between fifteen and thirty acres. From him come the perquisites born of necessity; but a comfortable tenant holding a large farm is no source of wealth to the agent. He can pay his rent, and with the percentage the agent's profit ceases.

Politics Mr. Casey has none, save so far as his own immediate interest is concerned. To-day he is in favour of a peasant proprietary. If Mr. Melville sells Ballybotherem he will out-Herod Herod in his denunciation of any measure that would interfere with the sacred and settled rights of property. When he was an attorney he joined heartily in the solicitors' league not to lend money upon any property that had been registered for facility of transfer. The registration struck at the dearest rights of the solicitors in their enormous charges for "searches." Now he is all in favour of a sweeping measure compelling the registration and facilitating the sale of property. Acknowledging no interest beyond his own prosperity, he will continue to sell justice and mercy to the highest bidder, and feel in his old age that he has done his duty to himself and his family.

CHAPTER V.

A GENTLEMAN FARMER.

MR. HYACINTH O'CALLAGHAN of Gurtnamona, or
" Hycy," as he is called by his friends, has never
repined at the fate that made him a farmer. From
the day when, in accordance with his father's will,
he took possession of the 150 acres surrounding the
small house of Gurtnamona, he has known no real
sorrows, nor felt the unhappiness of an unsatisfied
ambition. Not that his ambition soared to heights
unknown to the average farmer. He wants a good
price for his horse ; a good profit on his heifers and
sheep, and he has generally succeeded in obtaining
both. When he entered into the occupation of
Gurtnamona there was a considerable amount of
tillage. But this did not suit Mr. O'Callaghan's
tastes. He has no intention, nor has he ever had
any, of being a slave to his business. He wants a
roof over his head, enough to share with a friend or
friends, as the case may be, and a good horse to
ride to hounds. So long as Gurtnamona gives him
all three he is satisfied. As to the difference in

results between tillage and grazing, he has never
gone into the matter closely, but has a general
conviction that as tillage requires more outlay in
labour and manure it must therefore be less profitable. Of questions as to the relative value of
manures, the best rotation of crops, the crops suit-
able to particular lands, and the amount of money
per acre necessary for their proper cultivation, he
is as ignorant as is his brother Tom, who is with his
regiment simmering on the plains of India. Hycy
soon turned the farm into grass, retaining in tillage
only so much as gives him potatoes, oats for the
horses, and some turnips for winter feeding.

This system has a twofold advantage. It gets
rid of the necessity for ready-money payments to
labourers, and relieves him from the drudgery of
superintendence. Not that Hycy O'Callaghan
would under any circumstances have condemned
himself to drudgery for the sake—as he puts it—of
a few shillings more or less, but he feels that the
farming that confines itself to the buying and selling
of stock is in every way a more gentleman-like
business. When Mr. O'Callaghan was left the farm
of Gurtnamona he came in for the lease alone.
His father had not considered it necessary to leave
him any money for the purchase of stock, and the
problem how to work the farm was not easy of
solution. However, the bank was accommodating,
and in return for the deposit of his lease in the
bank-safe, he has been granted permission to over-

draw his account permanently to an amount sufficient to stock the farm. From that day to this
Mr. O'Callaghan has never quite known if he was
solvent at any given moment; but he has bought
and sold, hunted, shot, taken his part as steward of
the neighbouring race meeting, and generally carried
himself with as light a heart as if Gurtnamona were
his own and no half-yearly settlement of interest on
overdrafts were ever entered in his bank-book.

Mr. O'Callaghan is a thorough sportsman. From
the time when he escaped from the nursery he has
devoted himself heartily to the destruction of fish,
flesh, and fowl. He has caught everything from a
"pinkeen" to a salmon, shot everything from a
wren to a wild goose, and hunted everything from
the mouse in the corn-stack to the fox in the gorse
cover. See him open the stomach of his first trout,
and, placing the contents in a glass of clear water,
note the fly most tempting for that day, and you
can understand one of the elements of his success.
He is a dead shot ; but as a shooting man his conduct is not above reproach, and his ideas about
boundaries are hazy. A certain off-handed carelessness as to the sacredness of his neighbour's
preserves has caused some irritation from time to
time ; and when he exterminated the covey of
thirteen partridges carefully preserved for Mr.
Lloyd's friends, who were to shoot the following day,
that gentleman would have taken serious notice of
the matter had a connection of his not been a can-

didate for the appointment of petty-sessions clerk and Mr. O'Callaghan's cousin one of the magistrates with whom the appointment rested.

But the true magnet that has drawn Mr. O'Callaghan and most of his friends towards the occupation of a stock farmer is the branch of his business connected with the making and selling of horses. Here he feels that his occupation is that of a gentleman. From the purchase of the two brown colts at Cahirmee fair to their sale two years after at Ballinasloe as trained hunters, the speculation has been an abiding source of pleasure. Their training was a pastime, and the profit on their sale more than sufficient to pay for his subscription to the county hounds, the pink that made so brave a show at the cover-side, and the incidental expenses of the hunting season.

At the fair of Ballinasloe Mr. O'Callaghan is seen in great force. Here his flock forms a portion of the acres of snowy wool through which crowds of buyers wend their way ; and the second day his cattle are to be found in the usual corner, among the many thousand with which the large fair-green is packed. Their sale is a matter of business, interesting only in its results, and the prices are settled in the main by the market quotations. But all his energies are devoted to the sale of the horses on the third day. Two years ago he bought that chestnut colt at Mullingar fair as a four-year-old for £80 ; now the question is what money to ask.

Only for that suspicion—a mere suspicion—that his wind is not quite right, the horse ought to be worth £400 as a weight-carrying hunter. It will never do to ask a smaller sum for him, lest suspicion as to his soundness might be aroused ; and yet too large a margin between the upset price and the hundred and fifty guineas for which he would gladly turn the raking chestnut over to a buyer might peril the sale. This is a matter of too deep moment to be settled by himself ; so two or three brother sportsmen are taken into confidence and consultation, when crafty plans and wily combinations are arranged that must succeed, only that they have for their basis the guileless innocence of some wealthy horse-dealer. The quiet little man, rather like a respectable butler with Puritan tendencies, who stops the chestnut as Mr. O'Callaghan rides him up and down the green, is not taken in by the reproachful observations of Mr. O'Callaghan's trusty friend, Billy Mulcahy, who ranges alongside when the dealer stops the horse, saying—

"Hallo, Hycy! Is that the horse you rode in the famous run from Corrig-na-sassenagh Gorse last Christmas ?"

"Yes, Bill."

"Good heavens! you are not going to sell the horse that jumped the canal at Ballytracy ?"

"I am, indeed. I can't afford to keep so good a one."

"Well, I did not think money would tempt you to part with that horse. Good-bye."

The pint of linseed oil given to the chestnut before he left the stable has not had the desired effect. Mr. O'Callaghan has been assured that for one day it will render detection of slightly broken wind impossible, but the placid dealer sees through it before the horse has galloped two hundred yards, and turns away saying he is too good for his money. Still, the horse is ultimately sold, on account of his jumping powers, at a figure that saves his owner from actual loss.

Mr. O'Callaghan is hospitable, and his friends, Kelly of Kelly's Grove, French of Clonlough, O'Malley of Stabletown, and three or four other gallant sportsmen of the same kidney, are always welcome, as he is to their houses. The grass that straggles over the neglected gravel of the approach, and the flowering dandelions that flourish upon it spite of passing cartwheels and horses' hoofs, show that neatness is not to be counted among his virtues. A scraggy cotoneaster, torn from its support against the wall, falls across the open hall door, but has been roughly hoisted to a level with the top by a piece of rope made fast to a wall-hook above. At the door lies Tiger, a good specimen of the bull-terrier, and two handsome Gordon setters walk in and out at their own sweet will. Mr. O'Callaghan's friends understand the ways of the house, and, having left their horses in the yard, have no fear of the dogs, who know them all, but walk straight into the room that serves at once as drawing-room, dining-room, and smoking-room. On the walls hang some sporting prints and a lithograph copy of the portrait presented to the master of the hounds by the members of the hunt. On the sideboard is a miscellaneous collection of old newspapers, almanacks, some railway novels, and a moth-eaten stuffed snipe of abnormal size. We will not look into the corners or behind the writing-desk, nor yet too closely under the dining-table ; for, sooth to say, Mr. O'Callaghan is a careless man, and never observes the little heaps of dust and breadcrumbs in which each leg of the table is set. If he did, Biddy O'Shea, who cooks his unpretending dinners so satisfactorily and attends to his few household wants, would declare that he was " no better than a mean prying Scotch steward, to go throublin' his head about little things in the house, when her heart was broke with work intirely." As to the cookery, even Biddy declares that " the masther " is reasonable.

"My dear fellow," Mr. O'Callaghan always observes to a person invited to dine at Gurtnamona for the first time, " I don't go in for any of your new-fangled, nonsensical dishes. I'll give you a good piece of corn-beef and a wisp of cabbage, or a boiled goose with onion-sauce. You shall have some ten-year-old Jameson's whisky, and we will have a jolly good song and a chorus after dinner. So if that won't tempt you, do not come."

Gurtnamona contains three bedrooms, two of

which boast of four beds in each. This arrangement affords more accommodation than would be
found in a coldly formal English house, and pro-
motes friendly conversation after the party has
retired to bed, besides offering many additional
opportunities for a handicap or a less complicated
bargain. Handicapping is nearly a lost art, but
Mr. O'Callaghan's friends acknowledge that no
man could more satisfactorily arrange an exchange.
He undertakes to bring a racehorse and a clothes-
horse together to the satisfaction of all parties, and
had no hesitation in handicapping Browne's broken-
winded mare with O'Connor's grey hunter up to
14 st. Both owners placing a piece of money
under the bedclothes, their host said rapidly—

"The mare gives the horse sixty pounds. The
horse gives the mare ten pounds. The mare gives
the horse seventy pounds. The horse gives the
mare ninety pounds. The mare gives the horse
thirty-five pounds. The horse gives the mare forty
pounds—Draw."

And as each produced a piece of money indicating that the award was accepted, the bargain was
declared struck. O'Connor was not satisfied when
he found that out of the puzzle of big sums twenty-
five pounds only with the broken-winded mare was
the exchange for his horse ; but having drawn the
money, he could no more declare off the bargain
than if he had permitted a buyer at a fair to place
mud on the back of his cattle after having named
a price.

Mr. O'Callaghan is not a drunkard, though his brother Tom, when home on leave, warned him that he drank more than was good for him. He certainly is not anything like a total abstainer, and when he rode the Bellman colt up the steps of the "grand" stand at Liscannor races, his enemies hinted that that extremely dangerous performance was the consequence of the champagne he had previously imbibed at the luncheon table underneath. But many young ladies present refused to regard the frolic as anything but an evidence of cool courage, while the delighted multitude outside the enclosure greeted the daring feat with roars of delight. At Punchestown, where so many old friends are met, he shares a goodly number of glasses, and when the "Irish money" is on in the right direction at Liverpool, he pleads guilty to a "night of it" at his hotel in honour of the success.

How the farming pays with so very little supervision is a mystery to many. In reality it does not pay in the sense in which a hard-working farmer would use the word. The rent is low, and the profits enable Mr. O'Callaghan to live from hand to mouth. He has been told that high feeding on the grass will make the pasture much more valuable, and stall-feeding with more tillage would greatly increase his income; but no cottier is really less progressive than he. Looking only for enough to afford him the beaten track of his amusements he does not contemplate any change that would entail greater trouble and possibly greater risk. He had some idea at one time of taking the farm at Croghan; but the herd, who as a matter of course went with the farm, bore so bad a character that he would not have him, and to dismiss him meant a deliberate courting of peril from which Mr. O'Callaghan shrank; so he gave up the idea. With the country people around he is a favourite: never interfering in local affairs or politics, always ready to give if possible a helping hand at a fair, and constantly looking about for young horses, he and the people are on the most friendly terms. He certainly got a bad beating returning one night from Knockfad, where he had been dining with the other members of the hunt. He was confined to bed for a week, and would have sworn informations only that in the handsomest manner some of the party who had waylaid him waited upon him and explained that they had mistaken him for young Mr. Blundel of Moyglass, who was to have driven home by that road but unfortunately went by another way. The explanation was quite satisfactory, and Mr. O'Callaghan declared that he bore no malice for the mistake. On the hill opposite to Gurtnamona a large bonfire blazed the night of the first day on which he left the house, and he duly appreciated the compliment.

Mr. O'Callaghan's politics are not very decided.

However, his cousin twice removed, O'Callaghan of Derrypark, is the head of the family, and as he has always been a Conservative Mr. O'Callaghan goes with him. On questions of home politics he is profoundly ignorant, but he has an idea that a war would be a good thing in many ways. It would, he thinks, raise the price of cattle, and might give his brother Tom promotion. He takes but little interest in the land question as a means to enable him to purchase his farm. He feels quite contented as he is, and would laugh at the person who gravely proposed an increase of ten or twenty per cent. to his rent for thirty-five years that he might find himself the owner in fee at the expiration of that time. Besides, Mr. O'Callaghan's passion is fox-hunting, and being convinced that peasant-proprietary is inimical to that noble sport, he is prepared to oppose it to the bitter end.

CHAPTER VI.

A PARISH PRIEST.

FATHER PETER MORRISSEY was considered a lucky man when he succeeded in obtaining the parish of Kilnascalp. The parish is large, and the income proportionate. The river that runs its rapid course through the "scalp," or ravine, from which the ruined church close by takes its name, affords excellent sport for the fishermen, and the surrounding plains have been the scene of many a hard-run course. Father Morrissey had not been installed in the parish for more than a year when he announced that the chapel was too small for the congregation, and called for the subscriptions of the faithful towards the erection of a new building that would not be a disgrace to the parish. Appeals published at home and abroad were assisted by a lottery, in which the principal prize was a pony phaeton and a pair of ponies, or £100. Tens of thousands of tickets at sixpence each were sold ; and between the proceeds and the subscriptions received from every quarter of the globe in answer to advertisements and personal appeals, so much money was collected that the small and unpretending whitewashed chapel, outside which, in sunshine or rain, knelt scores of people every Sunday who could not gain admission by reason of the closely packed crowd within, has been replaced by a large and handsome structure of hammered stone; while a comfortable glebe-house close by affords more ample accommodation than the modest two rooms in a farmhouse heretofore occupied by the parish priest.

Father Morrissey's education has not been conducive to breadth of view. As a boy, sitting by the fireside in his father's farmhouse, he listened to stories of the days of the cruel penal laws, or joined in cursing the memory of the brutal yeomanry* whose atrocities preceded the rebellion

---

* "It happened that the barony of Carbery, in the county of Kildare, was proclaimed under the Insurrection Act, and a camp established in it, which was occupied by the Fraser Fencibles. One evening the commanding officer, a Captain Fraser, returning to camp from Maynooth, where he had dined and drank freely, passed through a district belonging to my father, which was very peaceable and had not been included in the proclamation. As Captain Fraser rode through the village of Cloncurry, attended by an orderly dragoon, just as the summer sun was setting, he saw an old man, named Christopher Dixon, upon the roadside, engaged in mending his cart. The captain challenged him for being out after sunset, in contravention of the terms of the proclamation. Dixon replied that he was not in a proclaimed district, and that he was engaged in his lawful business, preparing his cart to take a load to Dublin the following day. The captain immediately made him prisoner and placed him on horseback behind his orderly. The party

of '98. He heard extracts read from the *Nation*, and ballads sung, all having for their burden the baseness of England, the slavery of Ireland, and the glory of revolution. Brought up on such

proceeded about half a mile in this manner to a turnpike, where the officer got into a quarrel with the gatekeeper and some delay took place, of which Dixon took advantage to beg of the turnpike man to explain that the district in which he was taken was not proclaimed, and that therefore there was no just ground for his arrest. While the altercation was proceeding, the poor old man (he was about eighty years of age) slipped off from the dragoon's horse, and was proceeding homewards, when the officer and soldier followed him, and having despatched him with sixteen dirk and sabre wounds, of which nine were declared to be mortal, they rode off to the camp. A coroner's inquest was held on the body, and a verdict of wilful murder returned ; whereupon Mr. Thomas Ryan, a magistrate, and the immediate landlord of Dixon under my father, proceeded to the camp with a warrant for the apprehension of Captain Fraser, who, however, was protected by his men, and Mr. Ryan was driven off. Mr. Ryan applied to my father, who sent me with him to Lord Carhampton, then Commander-in-Chief in Ireland. We were accompanied by Colonel (afterwards General Sir George) Cockburn ; and Mr. Ryan having produced the warrant and Colonel Cockburn having pointed out the provision of the Mutiny Act bearing upon the case, we formally demanded the body of Fraser, which his lordship refused to surrender. At the next assizes Captain Fraser marched into Athy, with a band playing before him, and gave himself up for trial. The facts were clearly proved ; but the sitting judge, Mr. Toler (afterwards Lord Norbury, who was at the time Solicitor-General, but sitting as Judge of Assize), instructed the jury that 'Fraser was a gallant officer, who had only made a mistake : that if Dixon was as good a man as he was represented to be, it was well for him to be out of this wicked world ; but if he was as bad as many others in the neighbourhood (looking at me, who sat beside him on the bench), it was well for the country to be quit of him.' The captain and his orderly were acquitted accordingly."—"Personal Recollections of Lord Cloncurry," p. 49.

literary pabulum, he entered the College of St. Patrick, at Maynooth, where, amid 500 divinity students of the same class, he passed through his classical and theological studies, and emerged to enter the priesthood with every prejudice of his boyhood strengthened ; profoundly ignorant of the world or its political systems, regarding the Church as the divine source of all human power, and himself as the respository of no small portion of her infallibility.

Allocated to a parish whose elderly pastor had been educated at St. Omer, in France, he found himself in direct opposition to his parish priest. Father Halloran was a placid and gentle old man, endowed with considerable tact, and abounding with good will towards all men. There was no house of any class in his parish where he was not a welcome guest, and his unostentatious mediation had smoothed many difficulties from time to time between landlords and their tenants. With the advent of Father Morrissey the sectarian and social calm came to an end. The people were loudly assured that in him they had a champion whose tongue and pen would more worthily and effectively secure their interests than would the soft words of their parish priest. The affairs of the surrounding properties were closely watched, and the walls of Ballintemple chapel resounded to denunciations of various people for various shortcomings. When Mr. Taylor threatened to evict Michael Garvey, who owed four years' rent, Father Halloran, an old friend of the landlord, rode over to see what could be done, and pleaded for Garvey, as he had often pleaded for others, until Mr. Taylor promised to consider his case. But next day a long letter signed by Father Morrissey appeared in the local paper, abusing in violent language a man who threatened one of God's creatures with expulsion from his holding. The next Sunday similar denunciations were used from the steps of the altar, and Mr. Taylor was dared to evict a tenant in the face of an indignant people. Of course a threatening letter followed this discourse, which decided Mr. Taylor, and Garvey was evicted. Father Halloran's well-meant efforts passed unnoticed; but Father Morrissey wrote himself into notoriety, and was so fully adopted as the people's champion that at the curate's collection next Easter the amount given to him actually exceeded that received by the parish priest.

Transferred to another curacy, his pugnacity manifested itself with enhanced vigour, until, having graduated in the stormy squabbles of parochial faction, he received his reward in the comfortable parish of Kilnascalp. Troublesome as Father Morrissey has been, he is filled with an honest belief that, as his quarrels have always tended to the glory of God, by the assertion of the power of the Church, they must be praiseworthy and right. Of every transaction affecting the relations between landlords and their tenants he has constituted himself the censor ; and while he has succeeded in disturbing the harmony that existed for many years between the largest proprietor in the parish and his tenants, it must be confessed that he was mainly instrumental in preventing Mr. Moran, the pawnbroker, who purchased a small property near Kilnascalp, from evicting three tenants for non-payment of one year's rent that he had raised 100 per cent.

Cordially disliked by the gentry of the parish, Father Morrissey as cordially dislikes them. They are Protestants, and heresy is an abomination to him. They are to a certain extent powerful, and power in other hands than his Father Morrissey cannot abide. Between them and him there is not one idea in common in the entire range of metaphysical and material subjects. From the glory of heaven to outdoor relief they look at the question from opposite standpoints ; and Father Morrissey has no difficulty in adopting the view that to counteract the influence of men benighted by a false religion the end justifies the means. Viewed in this light, the entirely unfounded statement made in his sermon, that Mrs. Morrison of Roundfort, wife of the neighbouring squire, who was in the habit of visiting the houses of her husband's tenants with a view to their improvement, and taking soups and other delicacies to their sick wives or children, had endeavoured to proselytize the women by reading the Bible and leaving blasphemous tracts subversive

of the teachings of the Holy Church, may not seem
a mere ebullition of meaningless mendacity ; for it
had the effect of putting a stop to that lady's interference with the poor and the possible increase of
her husband's popularity. Not that Father Morrissey himself has ever attended to the physical
wants of poor people. Living by the dues collected
from even the poorest houses, his own poverty is
as much an article of faith as the intercession of
saints ; and an acknowledgment that his means
were more than his necessities would deprive him
of the small subscriptions of the many poor that
make up so large a portion of his income.

The days of Christmas and Easter collections are
the busiest Sundays of the year. At these times the
heads of families in the parish of Kilnascalp are all
supposed to attend mass, after which the collection
of Father Morrissey's dues is proceeded with. One
by one the parishioners advance and lay their contributions on the plate, while Father Morrissey
declares aloud the sum deposited :—" Michael Egan
—one pound. Martin Fruen, with one hundred
acres of land—one pound. Just twopence an acre!
William Slattery, ten acres—ten shillings. Mary
Finnegan, a widow with eight children and five
acres of land—six shillings. Verily I say unto you,
that this poor widow has cast more in than all they
that have cast into the plate. John Sweeney "
(Fruen's bitterest enemy) " seventy acres—three
pounds. I am glad to feel that John Sweeney is

more liberal than some who would have no hesitation in robbing Holy Church of her dues, and leaving their priest in want."

An interruption from Martin Fruen, who returns to the altar steps and says, " I beg your pardon, Father Peter, but I forgot to say that I have an acre of meadow for your reverence."

" Thank you, Martin. I thought you must have forgotten "—and so on.

The rich man pays his pounds, the poor his shillings ; and even the beggar, who locks his cabin by day while he roams the country in search of charity, contributes his mite. For weeks beforehand every sermon has contained references to the coming collection. Threatened and flattered by turns, the parishioners are reminded that not alone is their salvation dependent upon the proper maintenance of their priests, but their pride as true men and Catholics ought to make them show that, amid all their miseries, they are prepared to make great sacrifices for their Church.

No one knows more thoroughly than Father Morrissey the circumstances of his parish. In every townland he has a collector, whose duty it is to collect the portion of each man's crop dedicated to the priest. From these men he receives timely information of an approaching marriage, and knows to the pound how much money is safely lodged in the nearest bank on deposit receipt. He is always ready to lend a helping hand towards a desirable marriage, and his fee of 5 per cent. on the young woman's fortune sometimes produces a sum not to be despised.

Father Morrissey is a stout man with a florid complexion, whose appearance shows that, however rigorous his periodical fasts, their effects are soon obliterated by generous living. His well-cut mouth and square chin bespeak determination; but the severity is relieved by a pair of laughing blue eyes and a nose of the true Milesian stamp. His innate love of sport has not been destroyed by his theological training; and for some years he added a little horse-dealing to his sacred pursuits, being a constant attendant at the nearest meets and the hardest rider with the local pack of harriers. Unfortunately, the bishop began to view his hunting proclivities with an unfavourable eye, and the good-looking colt that he bought from John Sweeney can now only be made handy by surreptitious scurries across country.

But if he has been forced by episcopal prejudice to relinquish his hunting, Father Morrissey has an abiding delight in coursing. In the sitting-room in the comfortable glebe-house, kept fairly tidy by a good-looking niece, will be found two greyhounds whose achievements are known far beyond the boundaries of Kilnascalp. Most of the country is preserved, but except the property of Mr. Morrison there are few places over which Father Morrissey does not boldly course. Many do not object. Some do, but what redress have they? Even a Scotch gamekeeper would think twice before he summoned the parish priest for poaching. The county member had a large property close to the parish. Here of course no preservation could mean the exclusion of a priest, and many a pleasant day has Father Morrissey had on the property of Colonel Mansergh, M.P., who cursed his impudence under his breath, while declaring that he was glad to hear Father Morrissey had had such good sport.

The fiercest battle fought in the parish was at the time of what Father Morrissey called the Bunbury Exterminations. Six of Mr. Bunbury's tenants lived on holdings so small and so miserable that they could never hope to be anything but paupers. They owed four years' rent, and yet their removal was a problem by no means easy of solution. Ultimately the rent was forgiven, the passage paid of the entire number to America, and a sum of money given in hand to support them on landing until work could be procured. This offer the tenants accepted. But Mr. Bunbury had to meet an opponent who would not have his flock scattered by any landlord, however tyrannical. Letters filled the papers depicting the horrors perpetrated upon a virtuous and contented people. The dying mother dragged from her bed of damp straw and flung to her wailing children was pictured in vivid phrases, and curses were called down upon the head of one who could so prostitute his power as to destroy a God-fearing people impoverished by his tyranny. Mr. Bunbury could not understand the meaning of this attack. The incidents were purely apocryphal; but that did not prevent his being pelted with stones when he attended the election of a dispensary doctor. Ultimately the tenants emigrated, the six houses were levelled, and six small springs dried up that had helped to feed the stream of parish dues.

This was the only occasion on which Father Morrissey ever fell under the censure of his bishop. The latter reprimanded him for his attack upon Mr. Bunbury, whose conduct he declared satisfactory. Father Morrissey had too long been victorious in his controversies to tamely accept the censure of his bishop, and he answered in a manner so unbecoming that the bishop exercised his discretion by sending two curates to share the glebe at Kilnascalp. This arrangement was in every way irksome; and Father Morrissey lost no time in making his submission and his peace, and thus securing the removal of the unwelcome and expensive assistants.

The National school of which he is patron stands close to the chapel grounds, and is a source of considerable anxiety to Father Morrissey. He remembers when National schools had not supplanted the hedge schoolmaster and extended educational facilities into every townland. He knows how docile were the wayward and unlettered people to their spiritual directors, and he feels too surely that the mental activity of to-day has seriously diminished his authority. The educational zeal of the Christian Brothers he looks upon as a mistake; but come weal, come woe, the die is cast, and now nothing remains but to confine the inevitable teaching to the narrowest and most orthodox channels. Three times has Father Morrissey endeavoured to turn back the tide of popular opinion in his parish; and three times he has been forced to confess that, instead of being the leader of his people, he is their very obedient servant. The first trial was perhaps the most humiliating. When the Kilnascalp branch of the Ribbon Society debated the proposed rise of Mr. Mulgrave's rents on the hill farms from twelve shillings to sixteen shillings an acre, the meeting adjudged him worthy of death, and began to collect subscriptions payable to the gentleman told off to execute the sentence. Father Morrissey determined that a crime so horrible should not be perpetrated if burning words from him could avert it. The next Sunday he spoke openly and passionately on the atrocity of assassination, and warned the foolish men who had banded together with the desperate purpose of murdering Mr. Mulgrave that a crime so horrible would not go unpunished. He spoke for Mr. Mulgrave, and pointed out that even though these rents were to be raised the tenants had held the farms for many years at a rent below their value, and gave some instances of kindly

F

feeling and charitable action on the part of that gentleman. The following Sunday his congregation was composed entirely of women, and an intimation was conveyed to him that if he did not apologize from the altar for the words he had spoken the men would consider themselves absolved from attendance at chapel, or payment of dues. The day of Easter collection came, and the money paid amounted to £3 10s. Father Morrissey recognized the logic of facts, and apologized if any words he had spoken had offended the congregation.

After that things went on smoothly as usual, until the Fenian conspiracy began to assume serious dimensions. This time he was backed by the power of the Church to the fullest extent, and denounced the Fenian society by direct authority from Rome. The sacraments of the Church were forbidden to those who belonged to the brotherhood, and its members were formally excommunicated. The young men rose and left the chapel, and on the gate he found a notice headed "No priests in politics," repudiating any deference to him in social or political matters.

This was a bitter draught for Father Morrissey, and as week after week passed by and his congregation consisted only of women and old men, he felt that he must lower his flag. By this time the snows of March had passed, the "battle of Ballyhurst" was fought, and the defeat of the

Fenians at every quarter an old story. An election was at hand, and Father Morrisey threw in his influence with the popular candidate. Speaking at a canvassing meeting at Kilnascalp, he reproached the young men for imagining that they had been deserted by the " Sogartharoon." " No," he said, " your best friends saw that you were engaged in a gallant but hopeless struggle. The time has not come, but it is coming ; and when it arrives you will find your priests where they have always been in the time of action—at your head, leading you to victory." Once more relations were restored, and Father Morrissey spoke of his people as if their souls' desires were in his keeping. But his eyes were opened, and he saw with sorrow that the young men had almost shaken themselves free from the teachings of the Church and were fast adopting a Socialist creed. " No priests in politics " had ceased to be a cry but had become an axiom. Father Morrissey is no Republican. The entire theory of the Church is based upon an attitude of submission to a superior power, and the independence of the lower orders is inimical to the maintenance of a priesthood claiming to rule by divine right. Hating and fearing Socialism as does Father Morrissey, the propositions embodied in the land agitation of 1879 are diametrically opposed to his principles, and when the agitation began he refused to sanction by his presence its immoral doctrines. But the twice-told tale has again to be repeated.

An appeal to a people's cupidity aroused feelings too deep to be restrained by the priests; so now Father Morrissey's voice is heard on many platforms, and once more he resumes his ascendency, and leads his parishioners as a horse leads the driver who cracks a whip behind him.

CHAPTER VII.

AN AGITATOR.

MR. O'DOOLY can hardly remember the time when he was not a conspirator. Even as a boy he has done his scout duty by watching the outgoing and return of the patrol from the police-barracks, and reporting "all clear" for the men who from time to time struck a blow for Ireland. On that wild, wet night, long years ago, when Constable Davis, of the Irish Constabulary, returned to the barracks accompanied by the two sub-constables with whom he had plodded along the roads and into the by-lanes for four hours, and duly entered in his patrol-book that he had found everything quiet, he would not have gone to rest so free from care had he seen little Martin Dooly start away from the shelter of the neighbouring hedge, under which he had patiently waited, blowing upon his half-frozen fingers to chase away the pain that made each finger-nail feel like red-hot iron, until the cautious challenge from the barrack guard was

followed by the opening of the door, and he saw
in the glare of light the three drenched figures
of the patrol re-enter the barracks.   Next morning
when the report reached the constable that Michael
Traynor was forcibly taken from his house, past
which the patrol had gone only two hours before,
and carded until the lacerated flesh hung in ribbons
on his back, because he had bid at the sheriff's
auction for Thomas Meredith's cow, that active
officer cursed his misfortune in not having proceeded on duty two hours later.   But Martin
Dooly could have told a tale that would have
thrown light upon the fatality by which patrols
have so often passed by the scene of an outrage
an hour or so too soon.

Grown older, the spirit remained that kept him
patiently in the bitter night under the dripping
hedge, and enabled him even to overcome his
terror of the old churchyard of Kilpatrick, by which
he sped, never heeding the white cross that looked
so like a ghost in the ruined arch, or the moaning
of the wind through the leafless branches of the
gnarled old elder-trees, but intent upon the prompt
conveyance of intelligence to the waiting party.
He became an active leader in the dangerous society
that was formed after the collapse of the Fenian
rising : "Mutual defence against injury" the burden
of its unwritten articles of association, and the de-
finition of the last word only bounded by the
revengeful imagination of the criminal, the idle, or

the unsuccessful brother whose "wrongs" are to be redressed or whose interests assured.

By this time Martin Dooly had developed into a clever young man, whom his employer found it advantageous to appoint his travelling agent. No man had more business to look after than had Mr. O'Dooly, who had assumed the prefix, after the manner of Irish patriots. As provincial centre, all serious matters were referred to him. He is a clever organizer, and objects to the hasty adoption of extreme measures before milder efforts have failed. When Paddy Bolton was waylaid because he accepted the situation of herd to Mr. Wallace, a "brother" having been dismissed after forty sheep had died from neglect, Mr. O'Dooly was very angry because of the precipitate action of the local committee, who sanctioned the waylaying of Bolton before a threatening letter had been duly sent to him. Bolton was murdered; accidentally, the boys assured their leader, as they only intended to beat him, but he had a weak skull, and it broke sooner than could have been reasonably expected. Mr. O'Dooly severely reprimanded the committee, reminding them how efficacious the threatening letters had been in other cases, and how safe. Of course, in such an instance as that of Dolan, who had taken the farm of which James Corcoran was robbed because a few years' rent was due, and had kept it after three letters had been sent, a notice posted on his door, and his corn-stack burned, there was nothing for it but the pistol ; and if Joe Brien, who came from a distant townland to earn the price of the job, was seen coming from the direction of the place where Dolan's body was found, there was a large wake that evening at which friends from far and near had collected, which would account for Brien's presence in the neighbourhood. James Mullany had a very narrow escape when he dismissed Dwyer, one of his shopmen, on finding that he had fraudulently appropriated forty pounds. Had he known that Dwyer was a member of the society, no change would have been made in his establishment. Fortunately for him, there were others of the brethren in his employment whose interests were dependent upon his safety. Before Cooney, who was engaged, could succeed in executing the wishes of Dwyer and a few of his friends, Mullany received a timely hint, and, communicating at once with Mr. O'Dooly, the latter had the matter amicably arranged.

Still, however pleasant the sense of power, the career of a conspirator is surrounded with dangers which are fully recognized by Mr. O'Dooly. Apart from the vanity unsatisfied by the life of a political mole, the society left him nothing to which he could look forward but the ever-recurring round of warning and vengeance ; of purchase of arms and their distribution ; of a possible attempt at open rebellion that his own sense told him must be

abortive; to finish probably by a betrayal that
might end his days in a felon's cell, or upon the
scaffold. At the elections of 1874 Mr. O'Dooly
first took openly an active part in politics, though
not on the hustings. His business was to counteract
the laziness or carelessness of "National" voters
and to ensure their attendance at the polling-
booths, even though the ballot has so fatally
destroyed the hopes of the fight with the landlords' friends so dear to an Irish elector's heart.
This he arranged by personal supervision and
through the exertions of the district committees
of the Vehmgericht of which he was the provincial
leader. Now that he has retired from the active
direction of the secret society whose councils he
so long adorned, and has devoted himself to the
"constitutional" agitation of the socialist propa-
ganda, Mr. O'Dooly feels more happy. At last
he has his foot upon the ladder that must lead to
notoriety, probably to wealth, and possibly to the
dignity of member of Parliament. Drawn by
ambition, and spurred by necessity, Mr. O'Dooly
is determined that if distinction is to be the reward
of violence he will not be found wanting. Indeed,
after the scenes in which he has borne a part the
wildest language seems by comparison but harm-
less sound and fury; and while he congratulates
himself that he has now escaped from the danger
of his former position, he still drops a word in
season to the brethren, when practical illustration

is necessary to show the determination of the people.

Sitting at dinner in the private room of a country hotel, after a land meeting, Mr. O'Dooly feels that he has not lived in vain. At the same table are not alone the priests and farmers who form the bulk of such social gatherings, but three members of Parliament, one of them a gentleman in whose society Mr. O'Dooly little thought a short time before that he would have dined and quaffed the sweet champagne of the hotel, to the exclusion of his native stimulant. His purse is full, and he begins to feel that a Government prosecution only is necessary to ensure his return as the colleague of one of the hon. members sitting beside him. He has already had the gratification of hearing that his speeches are noted carefully, and that he is regarded as a dangerous man. This has secured his position as one of the regular staff of organizers, with a share of the profits, and his contributions to the literature of the agitation have been accepted in English and American papers. As a speaker Mr. O'Dooly is impassioned, and his command of language would astonish an Englishman with the same educational opportunities. Putting aside with lofty contempt the peddling accuracy of little minds, he boldly trusts to his imagination for his facts, producing pictures of tyranny and oppression that almost draw tears from his own eyes as he delivers upon them fervid speeches—accentuated by cries from his audience of "Down with the land robbers!" "Give them an ounce of lead!" He was one of the first who planned the organized resistance to the payment of rent. Not that he believes the people will long resist the temptation to take any vacant farms that can be obtained. He knows that his own brother John is anxious to add to his farm that five acres from which Peter Slattery was evicted, and he is a fair specimen of the average farmer. But the principle that no vacant farm is to be taken if the former tenant has been evicted is one that takes hold of the people, and offers more prospect of protracted agitation than would any other Irish cry. Repeal, Home Rule, education, readjustment of taxation, are so many sounding words that mean nothing to the average peasant. But "The land for the people" is a cry that all can understand ; and the volley fired into the house of the bailiff who at his master's request took Bryan Kelly's farm, surrendered when five years' rent remained unpaid, has been accepted as a hint, not less strong because of Kelly's miraculous escape, that for the present vacant farms had better remain without a tenant. Mr. O'Dooly has watched with keen interest the struggle between the law and the people. Having advised resistance to the service of processes or writs, he excels himself in his denunciation of the Government which, thirsting for the lives of the people, has sent large bodies of armed constabulary to enable the process-server to perform his " iniquitous duty." " Men of Ballymacswiney," he said to the crowds assembled at that village, " behold the blood of your women upon the reeking bayonets of the infuriated police. Rack-rented, down-trodden, starving, with crops destroyed, and the skeleton hand of famine visible upon the pinched faces of your little children, the land robber, who squanders in licentious orgies the fruits of your labour, calls for his accursed rent where there is none to give ; and the British Government, true to its bloody principles, answers with fire and sword your wail for succour." This is all pure imagination—no famine-stricken child and no licentious tyrant being producible for many a mile round Ballymacswiney at any rate ; but the speech was a good speech, and the speaker's assistance to the cause was well worth the £30 that fell to his share for " personal expenses " from the funds subscribed by the well-clad peasantry, whose healthy faces, violent mottoes, and martial array but ill accorded with the solemn pronouncement that they were starving slaves.

Mr. O'Dooly's friends, among whom may now be reckoned the advanced Home Rule members of the counties in which his services as a speaker have been in such constant requisition, declare that he is animated by a burning patriotism. But, in reality, the keynote of his character is uncompromising O'Doolyism. He owes his present success to his own unscrupulous intelligence, and the measure of his violence is what he considers his personal interests. He certainly satisfies the party with which he acts by a hearty hatred of England. But if he saw his way to his material benefit by adopting a different view he is not above conviction. So long as the present agitation lasts in Ireland, the round sum already accumulated in the bank on deposit receipt will steadily increase, and after the agitation has ceased to be profitable here, a lecturing tour in America or the Irish correspondence of an American paper is open to him. If he is so fortunate as to be prosecuted for sedition at home, twelve months in gaol will not be too much to suffer for the parliamentary career, with all its infinite possibilities, that will certainly follow ; and when by active wits and frugal living he has accumulated sufficient money to enable him to invest in a small property in his native country, he will confidently call upon the Government he has so often maligned to protect him in the exercise to the bitter end of the legal rights he may have acquired over the unfortunate tenants living upon the property he has purchased.

.

CHAPTER VIII.

A HOME RULER.

MR. O'CARROLL is a sentimentalist from the crown of his head to the sole of his foot. Blessed with sufficient of the world's goods to enable him to stare the baker, butcher, and draper in the face, and to walk into the local bank with unquickened pulse, he is still an unhappy man, and sorely tries the patience of his wife. He may thank that good lady that he was not more prominent in the Fenian rising, which, so far as it went, was in accordance with his principles—being an open attack upon police barracks defended by armed men. That no private house was interfered with is still a subject of pride with Mr. O'Carroll, who often tells the story of the parson's guns, surrendered in obedience to a civil request, and found on the doorstep, honestly returned, after the unsuccessful attack upon the neighbouring police barrack.

Mr. O'Carroll is saturated with dislike to England, and puts aside as a criminal weakness any idea that she may be actuated by feelings of justice

or mercy. Ireland's well-being, he holds, stops
short at the Union, and he refuses to see that any
prosperity has visited the Green Isle since that
political espousal. He remembers the horrors of
1848, and is quite clear that they were brought
about by England, and prolonged that a people
who would not acknowledge themselves subdued
might be starved to submission. He knows nothing
of political economy, and rejects with impatient
contempt the theory that the famine was the inevitable consequence of a rapidly increasing population
overcoming a food supply so cheap and abundant
that its failure left nothing behind. Fed from the
columns of the *Nation*, Mr. O'Carroll's mind cannot
acknowledge that any good thing can come out of
any country in Europe save France, Austria, and
Spain. There the banished sons of Ireland were
received by monarchs glad to secure recruits so
stalwart and fresh from hard-fought fields ; and
that two hundred years had passed since that wholesale exile of Irish soldiers is not counted by Mr.
O'Carroll when repeating his indictment against
the hereditary foe. He little knows that he has
inherited his perseverance from a sturdy Cromwel-
lian soldier, to whom he owes a portion of his
physique as well as of his force of character. He
has read the ringing ballads and stirring poems of
Davis, Williams, Sliabh Cuilinn, and others who
before '48 contributed to the poetry of the *Nation*,
until the flashing brand and glittering pike seem

Heaven-sent weapons by which alone Ireland can hope to win her way to happiness, to freedom, and to glory. Mr. O'Carroll is as free as any man in the civilized world. He can go and come without question; embark in any business he pleases; speak his mind openly; read his sentiments still more forcibly expressed in the newspaper of his heart. He can be married where and when he pleases, untrammelled by the restrictions as to times and places that bind his Protestant countrymen. He is protected, and his property watched by the police, without costing him one penny; and if he is injured, the prosecution is conducted by the Crown, not alone at no cost to him, but even his personal expenses are defrayed by the public. Yet he hugs the chain his fancy has forged, and cries with all his heart, "How long, O Lord, how long?" "What!" he exclaimed, in answer to an observation that England appeared anxious to give a full measure of justice to Ireland. "Will she give us back our woollen trade of which she robbed us? Will she restore the looms to the homes in the south and west of Ireland? Will she cease to pile taxation upon our whisky trade? Will she give us back our glorious Parliament in College Green? No, sir. England is the same brutal tyrant that she has ever been, and is determined to quench our nationality and prevent our prosperity, if she can." It is no good to point around, and draw attention to the improvement everywhere apparent even within

twenty years; to quote statistics of the great
increase of prosperity, agricultural and commercial ;
to point to the thirty millions safely deposited in
the Irish banks almost entirely by the tenant-
farmers. Mr. O'Carroll's Ireland is the weeping
Erin with the broken harp, and he will not accept
the dame who, putting aside her damaged instru-
ment, has stifled her sorrow and gone about her
daily duties. As he looks at the Bank of Ireland,
and sighs for the return of the Parliament, he never
contemplates a return of the Parliament whose loss
he wails. That collection of Protestants would
stink in his nostrils if the Irish Parliament were
restored to its old form ; and when Mr. O'Carroll
speaks so effectively for Home Rule he means the
grant of a separate Parliament for Ireland in which
the Catholic majority shall have all political power
granted to them, as a legitimate concession to the
Catholic minority of a United Kingdom. When
Mr. Butt's scheme of Home Rule was proposed Mr.
O'Carroll accepted it, and kept well within Constitutional lines in his advocacy of the measure. He
was one of the committee that deliberately chose a
Protestant candidate pledged to Mr. Butt's principles,
in opposition to one of his own faith. Such moder-
ation must, he argued, have its effect in the attempt
to induce the British Parliament to grant the
measure, or the Protestants of the North of Ireland
to combine in seeking for it ; and he deprecated
the Northern bigotry that nailed to the mast the

G

Union Jack as a protest against Catholic ascendency, and answered with Orange intolerance the
cry of Home Rule.   That visit to London—as one
of the witnesses for the projected company to supply
the town of Derrymacgeoghegan with bog water—
confirmed his views on the necessity for home legislation.   After a hard fight the bill was rejected.
The costs of both sides amounted to over £2000,
and Mr. O'Carroll waxes wrath over so unnecessary
an expenditure ; as, had the case been heard in
Dublin, not only would the bog water bill probably
have been secured, but the battle would have been
fought for one quarter of the money.   In this irritation Mr. O'Carroll only echoes the feelings of
more loyal men, who object to sinking their time
and money in the metropolitan maelstrom, while a
satisfactory and inexpensive tribunal sitting in
Dublin is palpably within the bounds of possibility.
Centralization has been made the theme of many a
diatribe by Mr. O'Carroll.   The iniquity of the
Government in drawing all official business to
London has been impeached in the most impassioned language ; and the board of guardians agree
with one accord that as an orator Mr. O'Carroll
would grace any assembly.   For Mr. O'Carroll is a
poor-law guardian, having been returned for the
division of Battlefield on Home Rule principles by a
sweeping majority.   Happily, in the union of Derrymacgeoghegan the issues on which the elections of
guardians turn are simplified by the elimination of

everything connected with the rates. The man who
would speak of a penny in the pound more or less
is a poor creature ; and if Mr. O'Carroll cannot go
to an alien Parliament at St. Stephen's, he can at
least show the world that Derrymacgeoghegan is
awake, and its elected guardians prepared to do
their duty as political censors. Even Lord Neverready, who presides so amiably at that famous
board, was obliged to bow before Mr. O'Carroll's
determination that his resolution on fixity of tenure
and free right of sale, of which he had given no
notice of motion, must be discussed before the less
important business on the books as to the expediency of granting out-door relief. Indeed, except on
such an occasion, or on contract day, Mr. O'Carroll
does not often waste time by attendance at the
deliberations of the board. Of course at the election of a master, matron, or doctor he attends ; for
if he did not watch closely, the small section who
pander to the prejudices of Lord Neverready would
probably sell their country by the appointment of a
Protestant or some equally undesirable aspirant.
In one way the noble lord is a true gentleman. He
never unduly interferes when the tenders are before
the board for tea, flour, meal, and other things.
When the ten samples of tea were on the table, all
in identical glasses, with the name on a piece of
paper beneath each sample, if the chairman had
noticed the piece of rough paper accidentally
adhering to the bottom he might have understood

the curious unanimity with which the majority of
the board, unversed in the secret of tea-tasting,
or "kissing," selected the sample submitted by a
cousin of Mr. O'Carroll's.   But even here centralization turns to a mockery the freedom of local insti-
tutions.   When the master appropriated fifty
blankets with other stores, and disposed of them,
on the matter being detected by an inquisitive
magistrate—pitchforked into the position of *ex-
officio* guardian without the suffrages of the ratepayers—and brought under the notice of the board,
the master explained that the whole thing was done
in a fit of absence.   His uncle, one of the most
respected guardians, proposed that the explanation
was satisfactory, and the resolution was adopted by
a large majority.   But on the minutes of the proceedings being transmitted to the office of the Local
Government Board, the guardians were directed to
reconsider their decision.   This was an interference
that Mr. O'Carroll was ill disposed to brook ; and
if the head of the Local Government Board read
that gentleman's speech in the *Derrymacgeoghegan
Vindicator*, he could not have slept easy in his bed
that night.   The board declined to request the
resignation of their master, and by return of post a
sealed order was received directing the dismissal of
that valued officer.

Mr. O'Carrol is an honest and devoted Catholic,
and by the light of his religious convictions must be
read every tenet of his political faith.   His political

creed may be summed up in one sentence—" Separation from England." When the disestablishment of the Irish Church was proposed he felt that for once an honest statesman had decided that Ireland must one day have her own. Though not just yet, the endowment would again be handed over to the Church of the majority, as it had been handed over before by Mary and by James. But the disendowment shattered his hopes, and betrayed in the proposer the enemy of the Vatican. The Land Act he accepts as a small instalment ; but while the ownership of the land rests with a number of Protestants he will never be satisfied. Not that he wants a peasant proprietary. He wants a country with a social system on the lines favoured by the Church. Fixity of tenure he desires heartily, for under no circumstances would he wish to see one man, woman, or child the less by emigration. He knows that over six hundred thousand people, almost all of his faith, are existing on patches of land under five acres ; and an emigration that would give them wealth and happiness is resisted by him as an injury to his Church. He believes that ultimately, by persistent annoyance which can be carried on in spite of any rules, the British House of Commons will be glad to get rid of an irreconcilable faction that only asks to be relegated to Dublin. Mr. O'Carroll hears from time to time reports of the intended abolition of the Viceroyalty. This he opposes with all his might, as the removal of the only symbol now left of the separation of the last century. He has joined the anti-rent agitation, as it promises the abolition of the present landlords, but he is not happy at the prospect. " Where is it to end ? " he asks himself, seeing no outcome of the people's passions save an abortive rebellion. Blinded by the presence of Protestants to the religious liberty ensured to him, his heart yearns for a Catholic Ireland, with a Catholic Parliament and Catholic Established Church : a country whose sympathies and political affinities would be diametrically opposed to those of the sister island. He does not see that, putting Protestant Ireland out of sight, the simmering socialism of the anti-rent agitation would under such a *régime* inevitably develop into an aggressive atheism with " progress " for its watchword, sweeping away men of his stamp, and rising against the tyranny of Catholic clericalism, as did the Catholics of France and of Italy. However such a consummation might ultimately operate by leaving England face to face with a people instead of a Church, it is a consummation that probably she desires as little as would Mr. O'Carroll, who will die as he has lived, in the belief that for Ireland's misfortunes the true panacea is Home Rule.

CHAPTER IX.

AN ORANGEMAN.

WILLIAM MCGETTIGAN was born fifty miles north of the Orangeman's Ganges—the river Boyne—from which venerated stream his father took the precaution of obtaining the water with which our hero was duly christened in the name of the great and good King William, who, if the toast nearest to his heart is to be believed, saved us from Popery, brass money, and wooden shoes. From the time when he was old enough to throw a stone at a Catholic procession on Patrick's Day the most stirring incidents of McGettigan's life have been connected with the annual commemoration of the two victorious engagements fought by the much-lauded and sorely execrated monarch. William McGettigan lives in a comfortable house close by the village of Juliansborough. The walls are whitewashed, and in front is a small flower-plot which in July presents a blaze of orange lilies. Indeed, the culture of that emblem is the necessity from which the flower-plot has sprung, and its effects are to be seen in the carefully arranged cut-flowers in the house and the general neatness that accompanies a love of the beautiful. The farm of twenty acres was purchased by McGettigan from the late tenant, who by careless cultivation had lost his money and fallen into arrears of rent. Three hundred pounds was a good sum to pay down for the good will of a yearly tenancy, but then the money was as safely invested as if in the funds, and the farm was worth sinking the money at small interest. Of course the money was paid in the Estate Office. The first charge upon it was the amount of arrears of rent, which was stopped for the landlord, and the balance was handed over to the outgoing tenant. McGettigan is a hard-working man, and though his attention to his flax crop while steeping fails in that scientific regularity that secures for the Belgian flax a higher price for what was originally inferior produce, he tills his land carefully. To a stranger he is hard and re-pelling, and his brusque "gude morrow" contrasts unfavourably with the pleasant "good mornin' kindly, sir," of a smiling southern. But under the rugged surface William McGettigan is as soft-hearted as a woman, where his prejudices have not distorted his natural character. His wife has him completely under her influence, and can regulate his movements except on the anniversaries, when, clothed with a purple or orange sash ornamented with curious devices, he rises superior to family

calls and devotes himself to the defiance of his
Roman Catholic fellow-countrymen. Mrs. Mc-
Gettigan is a native of Tipperary, and her marriage
illustrates the practical measures by which the
Presbyterian body manages to preserve its small
isolated congregations from absorption into the
mass of surrounding Catholics. The clergyman of
Mrs. McGettigan's parish communicated to some
of his friends in the north that a husband was
required for the original of the enclosed photograph,
who had a fortune of £100. In due course Mc-
Gettigan, who had just then decided upon marrying and wanted a wife with a little money, went
on a visit to the manse in Tipperary, and returned
with his bride.

The village of Juliansborough is a well-known
Protestant stronghold; and though a Roman
Catholic chapel stands about half a mile away, no
one of that benighted faith would have the audacity
to pass through the village to his devotions during
the month of July. One Catholic family has lived
in Juliansborough for many years, and one only;
and the consensus of Orange opinion (for every
man is an Orangeman) is that no other member of
that faith shall ever be permitted to obtain a foot-
ing in the village. However, to show that there is
no bigotry, the men each year assemble and reap
the crops of the one intruder. The principles of
the Orange Society are " civil and religious liberty,"
and McGettigan flatters himself that he adopts

them to the fullest extent.   Episcopacy he regards
with great disfavour, and Methodism is not to his
liking ; but both supply true and loyal members
to Orangeism.   He is therefore prepared to con-
cede to them the fullest discretion in their form of
worship and exercise of their civil rights.   But
with " Papishers " it is a different thing.   That every
one of these followers of the Scarlet Woman is
predestined to eternal predition is as firm an article
of belief with William McGettigan as that the
evening and the morning were the first day ; and
he feels that in doing all that in him lies to
obstruct the religious practices of Popery and
otherwise make the lives of the Papishers a burden
to them he is simply doing his duty as a good
citizen.   Still, for eleven months McGettigan's
hostility is torpid.   On Patrick's Day, indeed, he
wakens up to the fact that the country is being
desecrated by disloyal emblems.   For a week
previously the lodge has met frequently in solemn
conclave, and reports of intended demonstrations
are considered.   John Duddy's announcement that
the Ballymacgarret Home Rulers intended to
march to the place where a monster meeting was
to be held with a green flag, on which appeared a
harp without a crown, and " Remember Emmet,"
threw the members into a state of great excitement,
and a proposition that the men of Juliansborough
should attack the procession to show that the
peaceable and loyal inhabitants were not to be

thus insulted with impunity, was only negatived
by a small majority, on the grounds that a proceeding so justifiable in itself might bring trouble on
the lodge from the higher Orange authorities.
That night McGettigan and John McIntosh carefully loaded their old Queen Anne muskets, and
as the Home Rule procession wended its way next
day to the place of meeting, two loyal protests
were sent from a long range. Fortunately neither
of the bullets found its billet in the breast of a
Roman Catholic, so the processionists confined
their retaliation to firing a few pistol shots of
defiance in the direction from which the attentions
were paid. The incident was one of those that
so often give a zest to the pleasure of these northern
outings, and as nobody was hurt nothing was said
about it.

Patrick's Day past, McGettigan bears no violent
malice against his Catholic neighbours. He has
even walked to market on more than one occasion
with members of that faith. But with the heats
of June his sentiments become less dormant, and
with the 1st of July sets in a period of intolerance
that for thirty days at least subverts his reason.
During this time a Sister of Mercy with a cup of
water in the desert would be an unwelcome sight ;
and a general inclination to wade knee deep in
Catholic blood is accompanied by a worship of the
orange lily as real as the "idolatry" that he so
bitterly condemns. On the 30th of June the

village wakes up to celebrate the anniversary of the Battle of the Boyne. The drums are then first formally taken out for the July campaign and vibrate to the time of "The Boyne Water," "The Protestant Boys," and other loyal tunes. Every evening there is now a regular open-air practice in preparation for the procession on the 12th, and McGettigan's heart swells with exultation as he feels that each beat bears a note of triumphant defiance to the Popish community living down the wind. Before the repeal of the Party Processions Act the men of Juliansborough, in common with their Orange brethren, were obliged to march without emblems. However, no Government could prevent a man from carrying a pocket-handkerchief, and it would have been a tyrannical interference with individual tastes if it were forbidden to have that necessary article as large as a cavalry banner and of a bright orange colour, with the sainted King William in the centre, mounted on a white horse. As the procession passed by some street adopted by the Catholics as their citadel, the processionists drew forth their brilliant handkerchiefs and flourished them in the faces of the cursing "Papishers," regretting as bitterly as did the latter the restraining presence of a large body of constabulary under arms. Now McGettigan has the happiness of staggering under the weight of an enormous purple banner which follows in the immense procession, the warrant of his lodge

reverently carried by the master and carefully
guarded by the lodge officers. The procession is
headed by the Union Jack, which flag, thus
honoured, is pelted by many a Catholic father and
brother of men who have faithfully and gallantly
fought beneath its folds. Mrs. McGettigan, though
very proud of the enormous assemblage of Orange-
men in all the bravery of their purple and orange
regalia, thinks the weak point of the display is the
music—if such a term can be applied to the two
fifes and fifteen large drums that form the village
band and find their counterpart in the bands of
other lodges. She cannot help contrasting the good
music of the large brass bands that accompany
the Catholic processions with the ear-piercing
fife and spirit-stirring drums of Juliansborough;
but McGettigan answers that King William won
the Battle of the Boyne to the music of fifes and
drums, and what was good enough for him is good
enough for the lodges that revere his memory.

The Orange sham battle held annually at Scarva
on the 13th of July is perhaps the pleasantest
outing that McGettigan enjoys during the thirty
days of fury. Here contingents meet from the
various districts, special trains being run by the
railway lines converging to the place; from six to
ten thousand brethren being assembled, armed with
guns and weapons of every age and every degree
of danger, accompanied by wives, sweethearts, and
children, equal in numbers to the camp-followers

of an Eastern army. The host is divided; one side representing King James's troops, the other the victorious soldiers of King William. The former for the nonce assume green rosettes, and King James decks himself in uniform and orders of a similar colour. At a signal the battle begins; and while the women open their baskets and make ready the refreshments, the heroes of the fight join in valiant assault or vigorous defence, alarms, excursions, and hand-to-hand encounters being the order of the day. As the battle proceeds with varying fortune, the warriors fall out from time to time to slake their thirst and increase their ardour by appealing to the contents of the plethoric bottle never forgotten in the commissariat arrangements. Of course the army of James is defeated, and the last act is invariably the hand-to-hand struggle of the two commanders on a bridge formed of planks thrown across the stream that runs through the centre of the battle-ground. Here King James yields to the superior prowess of his Orange antagonist, and is made a prisoner: when, surrounded by guards with drawn swords and followed by King William on a white horse, he is taken to Scarva. Here in the public-houses victors and vanquished join heartily in drinking the glorious, pious, and immortal memory of the great and good King William, coupled with many contingent misfortunes to the "Papishers" and degrading uses for their remains; which are not alone to be

rammed, jammed, and crammed into the great gun
of Athlone, but their bones to be converted into
"sparrowbills" with which to tack on the soles of
Protestant boots.

McGettigan has a strong sense of his rights, and
even during his mad month an instinctive leaning
towards law and order. If a crime not connected
with Orangeism has been committed, he is prepared
to come forward and assist the police in every way
in his power; and under ordinary circumstances
the constabulary may always count upon his active
assistance if some of the wilder spirits kick over
the traces: but should the interests of Orangeism
require it, he is prepared to accept the consequences
of flat perjury. The clergyman of his church has
a certain amount of influence with him, but it is in
exact proportion to that pastor's attitude towards
the Orange society. The basis of his faith is the
warrant and rules of his lodge; and, while cursing
his Roman Catholic opponents, he never imagines
that his religion is as much a religion of hatred as
the gloomy frenzy of the Puritans or the tribal
ferocity of the ancient Jews. He has a great
respect for the old lords of the soil, but a poor
opinion of the manufacturers, be they ever so rich.
With the former there have been no clashing
interests, while his brothers look upon their em-
ployers in Glasgow and Belfast—between which
towns they oscillate—as their natural enemies.
With the agitation set on foot in the west of Ireland

McGettigan has but little sympathy. If it were a mere question of tenant *versus* landlord, he would probably think with his order, as he is shrewd enough to see that the bestowal of the fee-simple of his farm upon him by the State would make him a richer man ; but in his mind it resolves itself into a question between Catholic tenants and Protestant landlords, and his sympathies follow sectarian lines. In his political principles he is torn by conflicting emotions. He approves of tenant right, fixity of tenure, freedom of sale, and vote by ballot. So far he is Liberal. But he votes with the Conservatives : for is not the extension of the franchise a Liberal proposal that would, in proportion to the lowness of level at which the line is drawn, increase the number of Catholic votes? and did not the Liberals disestablish the Church that seemed to McGettigan an evidence of Protestant ascendency that gratified his vanity and assented to the principles of the Orange Society, in which all sections of Protestants could meet on common ground? McGettigan calls himself a thorough loyalist, but his feelings towards England are identical with his attitude towards the Church. He is loyal to Protestant England, because she represents to him Protestantism *versus* Popery. If she became Roman Catholic he would hate her with all his heart ; and if she grants Home Rule he will vote for the removal of the Union Jack from Orange processions. Even the grant of

denominational education is a bitter blow, though
he would die rather than send his own children to
a school in which Catholic principles are pre-
dominant. But, while he cordially hates the
Catholics for the love of God, and thinks that a
religious war in Ireland would not be all evil, he is
content in the main to do his duty as an honest
citizen and to give as little trouble to the Government as any one of her Majesty's Irish subjects.

CHAPTER X.

A SUCCESSFUL SHOPKEEPER.

MR. O'DOWD emerged from the quarter sessions court with a beaming face when the magistrates granted a publican's licence to him years ago. Hitherto he had struggled for a time as a draper, but found that his shop hardly paid its expenses, and offered no hope of ever securing an independence. But with the grant of a licence everything was changed. Mr. O'Dowd's friends and relations made it a point of honour to go in on market days and take a glass or two for the good of the house, and when Biddy Shea had taken a glass of raw young whisky she looked with different eyes at the shawl so temptingly offered for her acceptance on credit at the opposite counter. In a few years the shop was enlarged, and by degrees every branch of a shopkeeper's business was to be found within the ever-increasing area of Mr. O'Dowd's general store. The purchaser coming in to the market could there refresh himself with porter or whisky; he could buy bread, bacon, cloth, calico, seeds, iron, and timber, without leaving O'Dowd's shop ; and as everything was done on a credit basis Mr. O'Dowd soon monopolized the business of his native town. The signboard was repainted, and " T. O'Dowd, licensed to sell spirits, beer, and porter for consumption on the premises," was changed to " T. O'Dowd, merchant," the necessary publican's notification being placed on a side door From the first Mr. O'Dowd recognized the advantage to the shopkeeper of credit over cash, and the £300 brought into the business by his wife enabled him to tide over the difficulties of the start. His system answered so well that he has never changed it. No payment was asked, but 15 per cent. additional was added on to the price of each article. Then compound interest and half-yearly rests soon showed a sum due to him that enabled him to obtain a large amount of credit. After the first year the payments began, and a steady average was paid yearly, the account being never quite cleared off. At length Mr. O'Dowd found his business in so solvent a state that he was able to show by his books that on a particular day he was worth £10,000 more than the amount of his debts ; so he prudently settled that amount upon his wife, and come weal, come woe, that money was thenceforth safe. His creditors found this to their cost when he made his first coup in bankruptcy, and cleared off his liabilities by an arrangement with his creditors for four shillings in the pound. Good an investment as seems his trade, for any amount of money, Mr. O'Dowd has always felt that in landed property is the only real safety. As year by year small plots of properties in the neighbourhood came into the market he purchased them, and at last he was declared the owner of the Owenmackenna estate, on which there was a large number of poor tenants. The rents had not been raised for fifty years, and an average of two gales was always due. Had the unbusinesslike owner made a clean sweep of the timber on the property, or increased the rents, or even insisted on the tenants clearing up the arrears, Mr. O'Dowd would never have found himself in possession of a property that would in his hands clear off the purchase money in ten years. When the tenants knew into whose hands they had fallen there was bitterness in Owenmackenna, and Mr. O'Dowd was not long permitted to remain in ignorance of the ultimatum, anonymously conveyed, that any increase of rent would be answered by a bullet. Mr. O'Dowd knew his position and his friends too well to mind that threat. One son was the Roman Catholic curate of an adjoining parish; another the dispensary doctor of that district. Between them he was pretty safe to know if any real mischief was to be apprehended and from what quarter. A hard man is Mr. O'Dowd, and yet so plausible that even the victims of his system of bookkeeping and his proprietorial views say there is a great deal of good in him. " No, William O'Callaghan," he answered to that heavily rented tenant who with his wife came in to remonstrate against the increase imposed upon his farm, " I will not take one penny less than the value I put upon my land. If you don't like it another will. But that is no reason why Mrs. O'Callaghan should be in want of a better cloak than the one she is wearing. Go down to the shop, Mrs. O'Callaghan, and get a good cloak for yourself; you can pay me at your convenience. I hate to see any respectable woman wanting her rights in the way of dress." Mrs. O'Callaghan has been thus duly inaugurated in the mysteries of credit, and in her Mr. O'Dowd has found for the time a stanch ally. Mr. O'Dowd declares that most of the land in the country is let below its value, and that the tenants are well able to pay double the amount if necessary. He instances the case of the townland of Bunnanubber, let in bulk to a village for £60 a year, and sub-let in rundale, Michael Connor holding five acres in forty patches. Having striped the townland and settled each man's holding at a given rent, the tenants found that they paid double the former amount, and complained bitterly. Mr. O'Dowd, knowing the Irishman's hopeful view of the future, said he would not ask for any rent for six years, during which time any one of the tenants ought to be able to make money enough to take him to America ; but at the expiration of six years any one who remained must pay up the entire arrear. This seemed to the tenants a good offer. Six years was a long time, and God was good ! At the end of the time Mr. O'Dowd demanded all the arrears. The tenants said they were ruined; but in two instalments the entire amount was paid, as well as the running gales of rent.

Mr. O'Dowd has not retired from trade, as so many would have done on the acquisition of so much property as he has bought. He is as keen a man of business as ever, and looks upon his property as a means for the increase of his business. When Paddy Miles was met wearing a new hat, which he had evidently bought in a rival establishment, Mr. O'Dowd ordered him to attend at the office at once and pay up his account for rent and goods. It was only by submitting to a fine of half a crown that Paddy escaped the threatened ruin, for to pay up his account was impossible ; and he has undertaken not again to break the rule of the property by buying anything in any other house than that of his landlord. It is unnecessary to say that the rents on Mr. O'Dowd's properties are much higher than on properties belonging to the old landlords, yet no tenants in the country make a braver show at mass or market. Mr. O'Dowd holds that tenants will cultivate up to their necessities, and only so far. These necessities are rent, food, and clothing ; and the land, food, and clothes being supplied by him, he has a fair idea of the amount that can be borne by them. Tom Lahy complains of being charged 16s. a hundredweight for guano, instead of 12s. 6d., which is the price in the open market ; but as he will not have to pay for it for a year the neighbours do not think he has any cause for complaint. When he is asked to pay up an instalment of his account, he will have forgotten all about that item. Nor will he suspect that his twenty pounds' weight of turnip seed really consisted of half that quantity, ten pounds being a cheap seed of another description, duly scalded and killed by the thoughtful seed merchant, that its germination might not expose the fraud. Mr. O'Dowd is strong on the innocence of the transaction ; for is it not a well-known fact that the people sow all seeds too thickly ? and the little plan only secures that seed be sown in the proportion advised by good farmers.

Mr. O'Dowd's best customers are the women, whose adornments form the greater portion of their husbands' bills, to the great injury of these patient spouses. When Paddy Malley sold his cow, and honestly determined to pay the four or five pounds that he thought his bill amounted to, he was sorely vexed to find he owed ten pounds ten, which was accounted for by the price of his wife's new hat and shawl, and the finely trimmed dress with which his daughter dazzled the neighbours on Sundays. Mrs. Malley did not hesitate a moment in ordering on credit the green silk hat with blue flowers and feathers and pink strings for which twenty-five shillings was charged in the bill. Who knows what might not turn up before payment was asked ?

And had Bill Grogan's daughter been dependent upon the money in her purse she would have choked with envy before she allowed that passion to lead her into the extravagance of ordering a bonnet at thirty shillings that must have twice as many colours and much wider strings than Biddy Malley's hat.

Mr. O'Dowd is not a poor-law guardian. That position would 'deprive him of the advantage of contracting for the food and clothing required in the workhouse. He has many customers on the board, and can command the acceptance of his tenders. The representation of a division he re-gards as an empty honour, the command of the representative a solid advantage. After the partial failure of the potato crop of 1879 he soon read the signs of the times, and determined that if money was to be distributed his neighbourhood must have its share. He has adopted the stories of famine to the fullest extent. If money is to be obtained, there must be a high bid made for it in the competition of destitution. He is an active member of the local relief committee, and he de-clares the poverty of his tenants to be so great that special applications have been made by him in their behalf. Yet his offer of a reduction of rent had a curious ring to starving people. All the tenants on Owenmackenna who paid up the rent to the 1st of November were offered a reduction of 25 per cent. As Mr. O'Dowd says that the tenants owe him from two to five years' rent, the offer was a safe business transaction to him, and those who paid have not been neglected in the lavish supply of meal and seed from the different charitable funds. Michael Heffernan is one of the tenants Mr. O'Dowd declares to be five years in arrear. Michael stoutly denies it, but he has no receipt to show. Mr. O'Dowd's business system is not calculated to encourage in his tenant the independence of the village blacksmith, who "owes not any man." When Heffernan went at fairly regular intervals to pay his rent, he was directed to the office, where he was assured that the amount was credited in the book and no receipt was necessary. When he went to claim the abatement offered for punctual payment he found that his payments were all credited for the general account of shop goods and the deficit debited to his rent account. Heffernan is growing dangerous, and it has become a question whether Mr. O'Dowd will not give him the abatement.

Mr. O'Dowd has strong views about public works, and has spoken sternly on the impropriety of offering charity to people who are able and willing to work. A large drainage scheme would be worth many hundreds to him. The building of a fishing pier would materially benefit him. Of course the meal account is a paying business. But half the amount in ready money circulating in the district would yield him double the profit, as the contract price of meal is low. He has borrowed some thousands from the Board of Works to expend upon the Owenmackenna property; and as he has let the drainage to the tenants, who are to be paid by wiping off their arrears due to him, the grant of money at 1 per cent. is a windfall making the years 1879 and 1880 not the least prosperous of the last decade.

Mr. O'Dowd is a strong opponent of the cry for fixity of tenure at fair rents; but though a landlord he has thrown himself into the agitation for a peasant proprietary. While he was speaking at the nearest land meeting, an awkward statement was made that he had fifteen processes for non-payment of rent in the hands of the process-server. He explained that they owed him five years' rent, but forgot to say how the rent and shop accounts had been manipulated.

Mr. O'Dowd is prepared to stand up for the sacred rights of the people. A national Parliament and peasant proprietary are the two planks of his platform. Nothing less will satisfy him. "I am prepared to sell every farm on my property to my tenants to-morrow," he exclaimed, knowing how empty were the pockets of the tenantry. "The tiller of the soil, rooted in the holding that he has made fertile by the sweat of his brow, is the end for which we struggle, and which we must attain." The cheering crowd does not give Mr. O'Dowd credit for as much sincerity as he deserves. A peasant proprietary would mean for him a ready purchase of property. He has too large an experience of the certainty of mortgages on small estates not to know that the acquisition of property by him will be materially assisted by the segregation of the larger properties around him. Besides, he owes a grudge to the landlords. Being, as he is, in a position to know who can pay, he refused to accept the plea of ruin put in by tenants on Sir George Baker's property. In due course they were served with processes and decrees were obtained; but when the bailiffs went to execute the decrees they were confronted by notices from the landlord, who had not called for his rent, that the rent was due, and must first be paid before Mr. O'Dowd's debt could be considered. This Mr. O'Dowd stigmatizes as a shabby trick. A peasant proprietary would prevent such a plan for cheating the shopkeeper of his due, and Mr. O'Dowd would have no objection to even the compulsory sale to the tenants of the portion of his property not farmed by himself, if it were part of a scheme that would relieve him from the landlord's priority and give him a fair start for repurchase. The redistribution of property would mean increased security for his credit, and the certainty of an ultimate accumulation of real estate that would one day place the O'Dowds of Owenmackenna among the leading families of the county.

CHAPTER XI.

A WESTERN TENANT.

MAT EGAN is considered by the neighbours to be a very snug man. His farm of twenty-five acres of arable land, with about fifty acres of bog attached, is known in the Ordnance Valuation Office as Lot 9 in the tenement valuation of the townland of Knockeenashinnagh, a name signifying the little hill of the fox. The valuation of the lot is £18; the rent paid by Egan £28, being calculated at £1 an acre for the arable land and £3 for the fifty acres of bog. About ten acres of the arable land is generally under crops. The remainder is in grass, the limestone rock cropping up in places, so that, stooping low, these parts seem only a mass of bare rock with tufts of herbage and fern peeping up here and there. This portion was valued by the Government valuers in 1851 at a very low rate, and the bog at a merely nominal figure, as all light lands and bog were valued at that time. But Mat Egan knows how surely his sheep will find their way to the rock fields where the sweet grasses spring

from every cleft and crevice, and where they grow
as quickly as if planted in forcing beds ; and how
in winter the cattle will abandon the withered
herbage of the coarse bottoms for the bog, where,
gingerly drawing up the black rushes whose buried
portions are white and succulent and from six to
ten inches long, they feed upon the tender morsels
and thrive better than upon the grass. From the
bog, too, he obtains heather for bedding the two
young colts and an ample store of fuel for his house.
He has therefore not complained of the discrepancy
between his rent and the Ordnance valuation.

The house and outhouses form three sides of a
square, along the fourth side of which runs the
rough bohereen, or lane, by which the house is approached from the high-road. The centre is half
filled by a manure heap ; and in the green, stagnant
water that occupies the remainder the ducks and
geese find constant occupation. The manure heap
so boldly planted in front of the door gives off no
pungent smell, thanks to the deodorizing properties
of the bog mould of which it is more than half
composed. This has been collected through the
winter months from the portion of the bog where
the refuse of the turf-cutting has formed a disin-
tegrated mass of peat. The patient asses, who sink
half-way to the knees, carry it in panniers straight
on to the manure heap, where the withdrawal of a
stick allows the hinged bottoms of the panniers to
open, depositing the load without further trouble.

Opposite to the house is the barn, whose door is never locked—for the crime of robbery is of rare occurrence, and a robber or thief would have but a poor chance of escape from detection. Beside the house is a stable for the cows and the horse, and at the end of it a shed has been made for the cart, the roof formed of a pile of turf which can be used as fuel if necessary.

The dwelling-house is a building of one story, in the cave of whose thatched roof the sparrows pick out holes in spring and build their nests. The thatch is much more comfortable than slates, being warmer in winter and cooler in summer; and though it has assumed a green shade from the moss that has begun to form on the old straw, it will keep out the rain well for the remainder of the ten years since the last coat was added to it. Of course the gable is graced by a plant of house-leek, which is the only insurance against fire that Mat Egan allows himself; but everybody knows how excellent a preventive against fire is that precious plant, and how valuable a safeguard against the designs of bad fairies.

The door in the middle of the house opens into the kitchen and living-room. At one end is the room occupied by the two sons and the servant-boy, and at the other the apartment in which Mat Egan, his wife, and his three unmarried daughters sleep in two beds, the tops of whose arched roofs are the receptacles for the unused lumber of the female portion of the house. On the wall is hung a small delft altar surrounded by artificial flowers, and before this the inmates of the room devoutly pray. It must be confessed that on the window-shelf is kept the milk, and the butter that has been made for market. There is plenty of room in the barn, but the trouble of going there with the milk would be greater. In the middle of the kitchen is a long table at which all the family take their meals, consisting of stir-about and milk in the morning, with bread and tea for the heads of the house, and potatoes and milk for dinner, with eggs added in the summer and autumn. In one corner are the roosts for the fowls— for fowls must have warmth, and the kitchen is the most convenient place—and on the walls are hung two pyramidal nests made of plaited straw, that the hens may lay in comfort.

Egan's landlord made him a present of a range with an oven, which was anything but satisfactory, as the turf did not burn so well as it does on the ground ; but the oven has been useful for the hens to hatch in, and Egan has too great a regard for his landlord's good opinion to discard the un-welcome evidence of improvement. In every part of the house dirt reigns supreme, and a few pan-niers full of the absorbent turf mould thrown upon the mortar floor of the kitchen would materially sweeten the atmosphere of that apartment. Mrs. Egan would not consider it lucky to see the house unduly clean. She holds firmly by the old adage,

"There's luck in muck," which is interpreted so literally by all the household that no member of the family would court ill fortune by washing face or hands before going in to market.

When Mat Egan succeeded to the farm he found it saddled with a charge of £200, being the fortunes payable to his two sisters on their marriage. When, the following Shrovetide, he found that the matchmaker of that neighbourhood had arranged a marriage for each, he was obliged to borrow the money from the bank in the neighbouring town. This compelled a Spartan simplicity in family arrangements, and precluded the possibility of indulging in animal food, except a little fat bacon with cabbage on Sunday. In time the debt was paid off, and the gradually diminishing bill was replaced in the bank by a deposit receipt, to which money has been constantly added, until now a considerable sum is placed to his credit. His style of living has never changed, except that within ten years he has added tea to his expenses, for which he pays 4s. a pound, that being the lowest price at which tea is procurable at the nearest grocer's.

In the entire farm there is not one straight fence. The arable land is curiously divided by tortuous banks, which, with the "grip" at each side, measure at least twelve feet across, the cart gaps being built up with loose stones when the crops are down. In one field are the remains of a similar bank now partially levelled ; but Egan has never thought of digging it entirely away and utilizing the ground for tillage. If all the banks were removed and walls built in their places more than an acre of valuable land would be added to the tillage, but Egan thinks the operation would be too much trouble. Nor does he consider it necessary to plough his potato soil or stubble after the crop has been gathered in autumn. His father never did it before him, and he does not see why he should be always trying new plans like those Scotch Protestants who have settled on so many large farms in the neighbourhood.

Every grip is filled with nettles and briars; the growing oat crop struggles with the perennial thistle, dock, and prassia; and the potatoes have a fight for existence with couch-grass, wild ranunculus, and other weeds of greater or lesser injury; but Egan is of opinion that the expense of keeping these crops thoroughly free from weeds would be thrown away. In spring and harvest he hires five labourers to sow, reap, and dig; but in the slack seasons he confines his attention to the tillage farm, to the collection of bog mould, which is done by one servant-boy; while such of the labourers as are not small farmers hard by, return to the villages and towns, where they try to pull through the idle time with the aid of the union. Of course what remains of the circular rath, forty yards in diameter, in the middle of the potato-field, has never been disturbed by placing a crop in it. Egan knows too well how certainly such an indignity to the dwelling-place of

I

the fairies—of whom he always speaks cautiously as "the good people "—would be resented.   As surely as the killing of the magpie that builds its domed nest in the small tree close to the house would be avenged by the destruction of his chickens, or the death of a cricket followed by the ruin of woollen articles left near the fire, being eaten into holes by the infuriated survivors, so surely would the first interference with the rath be followed by some misfortune to his family.

Egan's eldest daughter Kate was married last Shrovetide, an event that was for a time the cause of serious anxiety.   Mary, the second girl, is more comely, and William Flaherty, meeting her at Mrs. Cullinan's wake, fell in love with her, not more from her good looks than from her general sprightliness and gaiety at the post-mortem festivities.   William Flaherty was an eligible husband in every way ; so the matchmaker flattered herself that in making the proposal she was certain of a favourable reply.   But there was a difficulty in the matter.   Egan determined that but one daughter must marry that Shrovetide ; and of course the marriage of the younger daughter would be an injustice to the elder.   Everybody knows that if the eldest daughter is not married first, she receives a " blast " that may injure her future prospects.   Kate feels that she would rather die than suffer the indignity of being chalked on " chalk Sunday "—the first Sunday in Lent—when the boys stand in rows at the chapel

door, their hands well rubbed with chalk, and
mercilessly clap the backs of the girls who have
been passed over in the Shrovetide matchmaking,
thereby branding them as rejected. So Kate must
be married first. The situation was explained to
Flaherty, and it was suggested that he should
marry Kate instead of Mary. This he declined,
and after much pressure by the matchmaker, assisted
by the girl's mother, Egan at length consented to
the marriage, undertaking to give his daughter
openly a fortune of fifty pounds and a second fifty
secretly, of which the priest was to know nothing;
thereby cheating that worthy pastor of £2 10s., his
ordinary percentage. Flaherty was also to have
five head of cattle from a herd of thirty that Egan
had on a farm taken by him as winterage. When
the bargain was concluded, Egan said, "Now,
William, of course I'll stick to my bargain, though
in all fairness Kate ought to be married first; and
a finer warrant to milk a cow or feed a pig you will
not find in Connaught. But if you will change
your mind and marry Kate, I will give you the pick
of the cattle, and if you insist on taking Mary you
must be content with the culls." Flaherty gave no
immediate answer, but consulted his friend Michael
Scanlon, who, on considering the case, advised him
to marry Kate. "For," he said, "believe me,
William, when you come to marriage there is not
the differ of a cow between one woman and another."
So Mary now awaits her turn, which will come next
Shrovetide.

Egan's life is by no means devoid of amusement. On fair days and at market he meets the neighbours and talks over local affairs. Holidays are rather a nuisance, as he is really industrious and does not like enforced idleness on a fine spring or harvest day. But a race meeting affords him the keenest enjoyment, and he looks forward anxiously to the annual steeplechases about ten miles distant. As for flat-racing, he considers it a poor amusement, only fit for Englishmen ; but he will stand all day at a big fence on the chance of seeing a fall, and shout with delight as the horses sweep over it. Were his fences twenty times as good as they are, he would gladly see them broken by jumping horses, and does not grudge the trouble of remaking them when he has had the pleasure of seeing the foxhounds hunting and the excitement of watching the fencing of the pursuing field.

But perhaps no day in the year has for him a greater attraction than the day when at the baronial sessions he fights his battle for a road contract ; for, like his neighbours who possess horses, he is a road contractor, and thus secures work for his horse during the idle time. He wants to secure the contract for the repair of five hundred perches of the public road running past his farm, and he has left no stone unturned to effect that purpose. Not alone his landlord, but every magistrate who is entitled to sit at "road sessions" is canvassed, and the assistance of the parish priest is sought to influence the ratepayers who have been chosen by ballot to sit with the magistrates. He is prepared to accept the contract at 8*d.* a perch, so he puts in tenders at 13*d.*, the 3 being so formed that if no lower tender has been made he can declare the figure a 5. Then tenders at 11*d.*, 10*d.*, 9*d.*, and 8*d.* are put in. If any other tenders are made for that portion of the road he claims the contract on the proposal immediately below them, withdrawing any tender for a smaller sum. The competition is keen and exciting, and he delights in the exercise of his cunning. Indeed, the entire business is pleasant, affording, as it does, opportunity for staking his ingenuity against the observation of the county surveyor, who might possibly pass as properly done some superficial repairs.

In years gone by Egan has listened night after night to the recital of fairy legends, having for their burden the rescue of some beautiful maiden ; or the adventures of some poor boy who leaves home to seek his fortune ; his mother's leave-taking being always the casting of a handful of feathers after him, while she cries—

> "My blessing go high, my blessing go low,
> My blessing go with you wherever you go."

And how, after thrilling adventures, in which he succeeded as often by cunning as by valour, he returns in a year and a day, having wedded a lovely princess, the invariable ending of the recital being " and if they don't live happy, that you and I may."

Now these charming and highly coloured stories have been swept away by the flood of education, and Egan satisfies his desire for news and forms his politics from the columns of the *Weekly News*, which is read by the National schoolmaster at the fireside to an attentive audience every Friday evening.   He was not certain that the English Government was such a curse to Ireland and the landlords such robbers until he heard the *Irish World* read, which interesting American paper informed him of atrocities committed in his own parish of which he had never heard before.

So far as his own landlord is concerned Mat Egan declares he has nothing of which he can complain.   His rent remains what it was when his father first took the farm, and in many ways he has been assisted by the landlord.   He has used these facts in his arguments with the National schoolmaster, whose political views are decidedly inimical to landlords.   But he cannot deny that on the property at the other side of the road the rents have been twice raised, until they stand now 50 per cent. over what they were fifteen years ago.   His two sons are enamoured of the doctrine of Socialism.   They are quite content to share the farm equally if their father dies ; and one points out that, although their present landlord has not raised the rent, perhaps when his son, who is now in the army, succeeds him the rent may be increased.

Egan's two sons have been for some time a cause
of anxiety to him. They are frequently out until
two and three o'clock. He knows that the meetings of the society he dreads are generally held
under the cloak of a dance, and he fears that sooner
or later his sons will find themselves within the
grasp of the law. He disapproves of the secret
society, and was so angry when Ned Massy, who
shot Mr. Brophy in the back when that gentleman
was driving past the houses in the outskirts of the
nearest town, spoke openly to his sons and daughters of his part in the murder as they sat by the
fire one night, that he ordered Massy to leave his
house. Of course he gave no information to the
police. He does not consider the murder any of
his business. Neither do the various people who
were standing at their doors when Mr. Brophy was
shot and saw the murder. And though £1500 has
been offered as a reward for information Massy is
perfectly safe.

Egan is not dissatisfied with the law, and
regards with uneasiness any projected change.
Fenianism he cordially distrusted, but his natural
timidity made him cautious about expressing his
opinions. The Fenians threatened to pike him
if he would not join when the time came. The
police intimated that any outrage would be visited
by a police-tax, and Egan declares that it was like
living with a pike at your back and a bayonet at
your breast. Until the clergy joined the land agita-

tion Egan distrusted that also. He is now, to a
certain extent, carried away by his family, who
have all, especially the women, entered into the
combination heart and soul. So far he has paid
his rent, though not until he was processed, as he
knew the danger of appearing to pay it without
pressure. The winter of 1879 has been a good one
for him, as Father Mooney has kindly put his name
on the list for relief, and thus saved him a considerable sum that he would otherwise have paid for
meal. Father Mooney has not been forgotten in
the Easter offering, and his kindness has borne fruit
in increased dues. But for the landlord Egan will
not produce more than half the rent at May, and he
is beginning to yield to the influence of his wife and
sons, who declare that even half the rent is too
much to give to a tyrant, who in asking any rent at
all is robbing honest labour of the land that God
has made for the people.

CHAPTER XII.

THE COUNTRY'S DIFFICULTY.

SEVENTY years ago there was not in the townland of Bohernasoggarth a better farm than the sixty acres then granted on a lease for three lives to Patrick Higgins. No clause prohibiting subdivision was included in the lease; and long before the original lessee was gathered to his fathers two sons had been settled on farms of fifteen acres each, and a third division was made for the husband of his eldest daughter, who came to reside in the house. Year by year, as families grew and marriages were contracted, the various divisions were further subdivided, until at the expiration of the lease Mr. Roberts, the landlord, found himself confronted by ten families, who claimed the right to be received as separate tenants. After some difficulty this proposal was accepted, but the original rent of £65 became £90 under the new arrangement. The Higginses are a wonderfully prolific family: and the Christian names are so often repeated that if you want to find a Peter Higgins of Bohernasoggarth

you must know if the man you require is Old Peter ;
or Peter Jack ; or Peter mor, " big Peter ; " or
Petereen, " little Peter ; or black Peter ; red Peter ;
Peter the lord, so named from a hump on his back ;
or Peter-na-puss, " Peter with the mouth "—a feature
so enormous that it might with reason be called the
mouth with Peter.

Malachi Higgins is the tenant in possession of
five acres of the divided farm.   The house in which
he lives was built by his father when on his marriage
that portion of land was allotted to him.   It is a
cabin consisting of a single room.   The walls are
made of tempered mud mixed with straw, and the
water that oozes from the rotten thatch makes slimy
patterns úpon their whitewashed faces.   In this one
room is a bedstead, raised about eighteen inches
from the mud floor, on which a feather-bed is placed
over a thick layer of straw, and in this bed sleeps
every member of the family : Malachi Higgins, his
wife, and the girls' heads one way ; the boys' heads
at the other end of the bed.   Before his father succeeded in procuring a bed the family adhered to the
primitive custom of sleeping " stradogue."   At night,
rushes and ferns being spread upon the floor, the
husband and wife lay down in the middle, the
youngest girl next the mother, the youngest boy
next the father, and so on in gradation of age until
at the extreme ends were the young men of the
family and the young women, strangers sleeping on
the outside of their respective sexes.   The bedstead

being raised so high off the ground affords a comfortable place where the pigs can sleep, and in winter the additional warmth supplied by the animals is welcome. The other end of the apartment is large enough to accommodate the cow and the ass, so Malachi Higgins sees no necessity for erecting a shed for these useful beasts. Malachi Higgins has had ten children, of whom seven are now alive. Each year as soon as the ground has been dug for the spring work his three sons go to England, where they remain until the English harvest has been gathered, and return for the winter, during which they do no work, and are ready to join any mischief offering excitement or profit. They bring home with them the worst vices of the lowest classes in England, and, having lived a gipsy life during the summer, sleeping in barns and outhouses, and far from their chapels, they no longer feel for Father Tom Ryland the reverent awe with which they knelt to him in childhood. They have never been to school, as Higgins could not afford the fee of one penny per week for each child. One daughter, Judy, emigrated to America years ago, and is now in service in New York. Nelly has married Richmond Monaghan, who has come to share the single room, and, by agreement arranged by Father Tom Ryland, Monaghan has one acre set apart for his own use.

As long as Higgins can remember, two acres have been under grass and the other land has borne alternate crops of oats and potatoes. With the one exception that the land has been turned up by the spade instead of the plough, cultural neglect could go no further in preventing the proper return of either crop. As the land is turned up the sod is white with the roots of bindweed or wild convolvulus, which propagates with amazing rapidity, and almost strangles the growing crop in its embrace. But weeding, except of the most superficial character, does not in Malachi Higgins's mind come within the meaning of agricultural operations. His fences, too, are covered with thistles the downy seeds of which are carried far upon the autumn breezes, and help to swell the army of weeds that consumes one third of the small farmer's crop. There is another cause that may account for the extraordinary differences between the yield of his crops and those of the great farmers of the district. He adopts the principle of selection and survival of the unfittest. Eating or selling the best potatoes, he gives the black ones to the pigs, and keeps for seed the tubers too small for sale. His seed oats are never changed; and he wonders that his returns steadily diminish. It is not then surprising that Malachi owes three years' rent, and already visions of possible eviction present themselves. Mr. Roberts has intimated to him that he must have the rent or the land; and Malachi has suspicions that his son-in-law, Monaghan, is trying to supplant him, as he heard that young man declare when coming home drunk from market that he could borrow the rent if he liked. Judy has written, enclosing a post-office order for £3, as that faithful girl has often done before; and, though she cannot exactly say what her father is to do when he arrives in New York, she begs that he will emigrate, and offers to send a free passage for her sister. Malachi sat one summer evening on the broken fence over against the battered cabin and its stagnant dung-pit, and he thought over Judy's proposition. If he could get Mr. Roberts' consent to sell the interest in his farm, he would probably get sixty or seventy pounds, which would be sufficient to take himself and his wife to America. But Mr. Roberts is a hard man, and would not allow any tenant to sell his interest; and as Malachi sat on the fence his thoughts went back over the years he had spent in Bohernasoggarth. Again he saw little Willy and Mary running out from the rickety doorway and amusing themselves by scooping up the green water from the dung-pit in a broken bowl, and pouring it over their bare feet. Nora rose before him, ragged and unkempt, her single garment a tattered frock, scarce hiding her attenuated limbs—dirty little Nora, with her grimy face and bright blue eyes, who long years ago crept on to his knee in that very spot one day when his work was done, and told him for the first time that she was "tired of playing." He went over the after-scene, when her lips were burning, and her eyes more bright, and he remembered with what agony he heard from the poor-law guardian that he could not have a visiting ticket for the dispensary doctor because he was rated over £4. How he had begged among his cousins until he obtained a pound with which to tempt the doctor to come out at once and save his child. How, unfortunately, Father Tom was dining with the doctor that night, and he could not come, and how next day the doctor arrived—too late. The three little ones sleep in the old churchyard of Kilmurry ; and every time he follows a funeral to that lonely spot, he picks his way among the nettles, that almost cover the broken tombstones and hide the exhumed skulls and bones, to the little grave, where, kneeling reverently, he offers up a prayer for the souls of those whose memory is still fresh and green. No : he cannot leave the place around whose squalid precincts so many memories cluster; and if Mr. Roberts carries out his threat of eviction, rent or no rent, there will be bad work in Bohernasoggarth.

Malachi Higgins cannot be called a good man. Out of his poverty he paid two shillings towards the honorarium granted to Peter Quirk for the murder of Darmody, the bailiff, who had served notices to quit for his employer. The service of the notices must have been proved by Darmody before decrees could be obtained ; and in the war between landlord and tenant Malachi Higgins regards the murder of a bailiff with as much complacency as does Mr.

Roberts' son, the captain, a successful skirmish in which the enemy suffered some loss. At the same time he performed a work of piety, as did Quirk, in attending Darmody's funeral, and no two men were louder in their denunciation of the cruel deed. One obligation Malachi has always faithfully performed. He has been regular in the payment of his dues to Father Tom Ryland, who now receives twenty times the sum from the subdivided holdings that his predecessor received out of the original farm. Father Tom will not see Malachi evicted without a struggle. The obliteration of even one small homestead is the thin end of a wedge that might ultimately rend off a considerable portion of his congregation ; and Father Tom Ryland is not the man to lose even one member of his flock without a struggle. To him Malachi has appealed, and he is leaving no stone unturned to excite public opinion against any eviction for any cause.

The Higginses of Bohernasoggarth are a strong faction, and Mr. Roberts has been advised to leave the country for a time, when he carries out the eviction ; but he cannot afford to go, and so the matter stands at present.

Not that Malachi Higgins's relations with his surrounding kinsmen are always amicable. Peter-na-puss, whose land joins his, asserts a right of way over a corner of Malachi's grass-field that the latter is prepared to resist to the last. Peter asserts that he has been going that way to his potato-field for

twenty years; but Malachi declares that he only
went by his permission, which was withdrawn when
Peter basely took sides against his own flesh and
blood, which he did by swearing the truth at petty
sessions, where Malachi was summoned by Bill
Maher for an assault and most justly fined—a
decision that he attributes entirely to Maher's
superior interest. The cause of the quarrel was
carefully excluded from the evidence of both sides
at petty sessions.

When Paddy Nash was evicted for non-payment
of rent, he appealed to the brotherhood to which he
belonged to see him righted, as the landlord would
not give him compensation. Why he should get
compensation, having made no improvements, the
landlord could not see, but Nash, who is penniless,
thinks he might have been allowed to sell the farm.
The society, true to its principles, took up the
matter, and a notice was posted on the door of the
vacant house that no person must take the land on
pain of death. Undeterred by the notice, John
Breheny, whose soul hungered for that farm, proposed for it and was accepted as tenant. Having
put a new coat of thatch on the house, he began
the removal of his modest furniture, and at length
everything was prepared for occupation next day.
But the society was not idle. It was determined
that the house must be burned, and Malachi Higgins
was appointed to carry the decision into effect.
The night before Breheny was to enter into its

occupation Malachi approached the house cautiously, carrying in a basket a lighted sod of turf,
which—first carefully preparing a place for it—he
thrust into the thatch.   Next morning the house
was a heap of cinders, and no clue existed that
could throw any light on the matter.   A special
police-station was established on the spot, and the
police-tax pressed so heavily upon the people that
some openly complained that the action of the
society was precipitate.   Breheny could have been
met by a party at a fair and beaten to death if
necessary ; then the neighbourhood would not have
been saddled with a police-tax.   But with such a
ready means of punishment in the hands of the
Government, the more cautious of the neighbours
deprecated these outrages, the cause of which are
so readily traceable and easily localized.   However,
most of the people paid up their subscriptions to
Malachi Higgins ; but Maher refused to pay, for
which treachery Malachi punished him by waiting
behind a wall, until, as Maher passed on his way
from market, accompanied by Peter-na-puss, he
received a crushing blow on the head from a stone
flung by Malachi, who jumped over the wall and
would have battered his head as he lay, only that
Peter took Maher's side, as his name was on a bill
for ten pounds which the latter had borrowed from
the bank.

Fortunately for Malachi Higgins, he is not entirely
dependent on the produce of his farm.   Each year

he takes a small quantity of turf bank on the verge of the bog, and during the winter the ass does good service in bringing daily a load of turf to the nearest town, for which a sum is received varying from 1s. to 1s. 8d. This is the main support of the family from December to March, except the contributions of the sons from the money earned in England.

To Malachi Higgins and his family the doctrines of socialism are received as a new gospel, and already visions rise before them of the division of the highly improved land now held by the Scotch farmers and the removal of these heretics from the sainted isle. Higgins has been promised a reduction of 25 per cent. on the entire arrear if he will pay ; but he has attended too many of the anti-rent meetings not to see that if withholding 25 per cent. may have the effect of forcing the landlords to sell their properties to Government for resale to the tenants on credit, the refusal of all rent must hasten the triumph of the agitation. He is prepared to join in whatever course the society may recommend, and is strong in his determination to keep a firm grip on his holding. His confidence in his power to do so, however, has received a rude shock by the sight of such a force of constabulary at the service of ejectment processes in the neighbourhood as precluded the possibility of resistance, and his sons begin to talk of the advisability of emigration. Malachi still feels that to leave Bohernasoggarth would break his heart ; but if the means for emigration were forthcoming he would not resist his sons' desire and the repeated invitations of Judy. Besides, the sight of one who had left in rags and returned one winter for a few months from that far distant country, clothed in broadcloth, removed the impression that from America there was no return ; and deep down in his heart there is a hope that if he is torn from the place so dear to him, he may one day come back to leave his bones in the churchyard of Kilmurry, among the friends of his life, whose crimes are counted as virtues by the warped morality of Bohernasoggarth.

CHAPTER XIII.

A DISTRESSED LANDLORD.

IF Mr. O'Hara, of Garrauns Castle, owed no money he would be in receipt of £700 a year or thereabouts. He still makes an effort to frame the arrangements of the establishment as if the property were unencumbered, which accounts in a great measure for the generally neglected and out-at-elbows appearance of the untidy little place. For Garrauns Castle is not so imposing a residence as might be expected from its somewhat ambitious name. A small two-storied house, there was nothing in its architecture to justify the magnificent addition to the name of the townland on which the house is built, except a modest attempt by raising the walls of the semi-circular porch to the top of the house to give that adornment the appearance of a castellated battlement. Once its name went near helping its present owner to a marriage with the daughter of a rich English manufacturer. It happened in this wise:—Mr. O'Hara, when a young man, spent some time in the neighbourhood

of Manchester, where he met the daughter of the
rich Mr. Plumrigg. He came, he saw, and he con-
quered; and nothing was wanted but the consent
of Mr. Plumrigg to raise the fortunes of Garrauns
Castle to a higher level than they had ever yet
attained. Mr. O'Hara honestly felt that in marrying
Miss Plumrigg, and consenting to accept her
£30,000, he was conferring an honour on that rich
but mushroom family not too dearly purchased
at the money; for the O'Haras of Garrauns Castle
came of a family tracing its descent for many
centuries. In the interview with Mr. Plumrigg he
answered that gentlemen's questions as to his property with such candour—showing that unfortunately not more than about £6000 a year remained
to him of the once vast possessions of his family—
that a ready consent was given; and he had the
happiness of assisting that evening at the Plumrigg
family dinner. Mr. Plumrigg was, however, a man
of business; and while Mr. O'Hara was engaged
with his wife and daughter in looking over the
most expensive things procurable with which the
Castle was to be refurnished, his inquiries of the
shopman indicating an order large enough to re-
furnish a wing of Windsor Castle, that gentleman
quietly took a ticket for Ireland, and found himself
at the modest railway station close to the gate
of his daughter's future residence. An Irish
jaunting-car of the usual country type was at the
station, the keen-witted but ragged driver looking

out for a possible fare.   No sooner had Mr. Plumrigg stepped from the train than Jack Rogers
seized upon his portmanteau, and was busily engaged in tying it on the well of the broken car
when Mr. Plumrigg appeared at the gate.

"Why," he said, "I cannot drive on a vehicle of
that description," as he looked at the car, which
was seemingly held together by ropes.   One step
showed signs of having once been painted ; the
other had been knocked off by a passing cart a
few days before, and the wood of the new step
was still unsullied by a paint-brush.   The harness
was a mixture of leather, wire, and twine ; and,
once off, no human being but Jack Rogers could
again place it properly on the wiry hack that waited
patiently at the gate.

"Arrah, don't be the laste onaisy, yer honour,"
answered Jack.   "Sure, when yer on the car you
will feel as aisy as if you wor sittin' on a feather-
bed."

"You know Garrauns Castle?" asked Mr. Plumrigg.

"Do I know the mother that bore me?" answered Jack, in true Irish fashion, thus indirectly
conveying assent to the question.

"Well, how long will it take to drive there?"
asked Mr. Plumrigg.

"I'll rowl you up in half a minute," replied Jack.
"Sure that's the gate there fornenst you.   But,
faith, there's no use at all for your honour to go up,

for the masther is not at home, an' there's no one in the house but owld Betty Murray ; an', faith, you must go in wid the hens through the kitchen doore if you want to get in ; for owld Betty is blind an' deaf, and sorra one of her would hear the Day of Judgment if it kem rappin' to the doore."

"Surely, my man, you make a mistake," said Mr. Plumrigg. "I mean Mr. O'Hara's Garrauns Castle."

"The divil a mistake I make, your honour. Sure, isn't Mr. O'Hara in England, goin' to marry a lady wid a million of goolden sovereigns ; an', be me sowl, I'm thinking he's the boy that'll spend them for her. Faith, when he comes home every man in the village will be drunk for a week."

Mr. Plumrigg returned by the next train, and no more family dinners were shared by Mr. O'Hara. The English matrimonial campaign having failed, Garrauns Castle was once more inhabited ; and in the fulness of time a marriage was duly solemnized between Mr. O'Hara and the seventh daughter of Gregory Coleman, Esquire, of Mount Coleman. Miss Coleman's dower was modest, and her £400 hardly sufficed to pay the expenses of the unsuccessful English tour and the wedding charges. But, the Colemans being people of position in the county and cousins four times removed of Lord Ballyheigue, it was necessary that a fitting settlement should be made upon Mrs. O'Hara, who became entitled to a jointure of £200 a year if she survived her mother-in-law, to whom that amount was then being paid. As years rolled on the O'Hara family increased, until it overflowed the nursery and took possession of the best bed-room. The expenses, too, increased in equal ratio, until even the falling-in of the dowager Mrs. O'Hara's jointure was only just sufficient to prevent a humiliating contraction of the establishment. With increasing years the expenses have steadily continued, until Mr. O'Hara is compelled to make the two horses do the work of the home farm in spring, as they carry him and his eldest son to hounds two days a fortnight in winter, and when not so employed still enable Mrs. O'Hara and her daughters to keep up appearances by driving in her waggonette. The coachman's coat and hat have braved the storms of many winters. The harness has long since been shorn of its enamel, and the silver has disappeared from its emblazoned ornaments. The waggonette has not been painted since the loan ten years ago, effected on an in-surance. But still it is a waggonette with two horses, driven by a coachman in livery, and Mrs. O'Hara feels that her dignity is sustained.

Mr. O'Hara's interest, insurance premiums, and instalments absorb £250 per annum, leaving the property worth on paper £450. But the tenants never pay up the full amount. James Neary owed three years' rent, and was ultimately evicted, Mr. O'Hara losing £45 by the transaction. Biddy

Russel begged so hard to be allowed for the timber and slates of a new cowshed that she could not be resisted, and £6 was deducted from her rent. Martin Scully's cow broke a leg in passing over an ill-made wooden bridge into the bog field, and three of his sheep died of rot, so it was impossible that he could pay the full rent; £5 was therefore lost on that account. And every year similar deductions were to be made. Then the agent's fees of £5 per cent. on the full rental come to £35, for Mr. O'Hara, like other Irish gentlemen of his position, indulges in the luxury of an agent. He says that he could not deal directly with the tenants, who require the sternness of a person constrained to refuse their never-ending requests for abatement on the plea of justice to his employer. When half the poor rates and the county cess and the income tax are added to the average shortcomings, Mr. O'Hara finds that his actual income is barely £300 a year in good years, and often falls so much below it that the produce of his son George's game-bag is a most welcome addition to the larder.

Mr. O'Hara keeps about forty acres in his own hands, and his smaller tenants are bound as part of the agreement under which they hold their land to work for him, whenever he requires their labour, at 8*d.* a day. This provision is readily accepted when a tenant is looking for a farm ; but once in possession they object to it strongly, and Mike Treacy, who took the corner of the deer-park for which several tenants had proposed, and who went specially to thank Mr. Coleman for his interest in obtaining the farm for him, now declares the custom rank tyranny, and when he does attend his labour is not worth one half the stipulated sum.

Mr. O'Hara is animated by the warmest feelings of friendship for his tenantry, whose families, with few exceptions, have lived on the Garrauns property for generations. He is always ready to assist them in any way where money is not required, and leaves no stone unturned to obtain appointments for their sons. He had serious intention of resigning the commission of the peace when, despite his strong recommendation, Bartly Nally's son was rejected as a recruit for the Royal Irish Constabulary, because he had spent twelve months in Canada; and nothing but his thorough Conservatism saved him from a radical transference of his political allegiance when Mary Flannery was removed from the position of local postmistress in consequence of ill-natured complaints of the illegitimate gratification of her feminine curiosity. If he could afford it he would like to improve the stretch of rushy fields gently sloping down to the river. He spoke to the tenants on the advisability of obtaining a loan for the purpose of draining that portion of the property; but, although the entire amount would be paid to the tenants for their labour on their own farms, they objected to the payment of five shillings per acre for thirty-one years, which increase would pay off the principal and interest, the improvement in the land being well worth the money. The tenants rather congratulated themselves when the plan was abandoned, and George O'Hara heard with equanimity a decision that leaves unspoiled by drainage his best bit of snipe ground. Except in the manner proposed, Mr. O'Hara could not afford to effect any improvements, and he shrinks from the trouble and danger of any increase of rent except with the consent of the tenants.

He is very anxious that his daughters should be fairly educated, but beyond a governess at £15 a year his means will not allow him to go. The accomplishments of the six young ladies are therefore elementary. As George is the heir, he remains at home to assist his father in mismanaging the farm, while his second brother is studying medicine at the Queen's College in Galway, with a view of becoming a military surgeon.

Many are the straits in which Mr. O'Hara finds himself from time to time to meet the current expenses of his education ; and when James Neary asked permission to sell his farm to Pat Toomey, who was ready to give him £85 out of which the arrears of rent were to be paid, he very nearly sacrificed his principle to expediency. There were so many things for which the £45 would have been useful. But Mr. O'Hara felt that to allow

the sale of a tenant's interest would be a surrender of proprietorial rights that might one day
diminish the value of the property; and he had
an idea that if Pat Toomey was prepared to give
£85 to the outgoing tenant, he would be prepared to give something near that sum to the
landlord as a fine if he agreed to let the farm at
the old rent. When Neary was evicted, however,
not alone did Toomey decline to give any fine, but
he refused to pay any higher rent than that at
which it was let before, at which rent he got it after
the farm had remained vacant for six months during
which time no other person had proposed for it.
Mr. O'Hara did not know that in offering £85 for
the "good will" of the outgoing tenant Toomey
was simply effecting an insurance against "accidents" that may possibly occur to the person
taking land from which a tenant has been dispos-
sessed. He was surprised that no other tenant
had made an offer for the farm; but he would
have understood their disinclination to bid for it
if he had seen £50 counted down in a crowded
room and handed over by Toomey to the man who
had been evicted eight months before.

George O'Hara has promised his father that
when he comes of age he will, in consideration of
receiving an allowance of £100 a year, consent to
breaking the entail, when money can be borrowed
at a much cheaper rate to pay the present debts,
and make some small provision for his sisters. He

looks anxiously for the time when he can keep a
horse of his own in the third stall, whose wooden
rack and paved floor remain as they were arranged
by his grandfather.   He has visions of making
money by buying raw colts and making them—for
George can ride as well as shoot ; and has no
thought for the beginning of the end, that will
come with the substantial mortgage to be effected
on his coming of age.

In the mean time the anti-rent agitation has nearly
driven Mr. O'Hara to despair.   Never having raised
his rents, he is nevertheless declared by Mr. Parnell
and his followers to be a land-robber, and the
tenants have demanded a reduction of 25 per cent.
on all rent due, and proposed that in future the
rent shall be the amount of the Government valuation and no more.   In vain has Mr. O'Hara declared
to a few influential tenants that a reduction of 25
per cent. on the gross rental, added to the large
deductions that he has already to pay, would not
leave him £100 a year.   They declare that they
dare not pay the full rent, and as leader of a
deputation to Mr. O'Hara, Bartly Nally told him
boldly that if he did not give the reduction they
could not pay any rent at all.   However, when the
others left the room, Nally took the opportunity
to say, " Serve me with a writ, your honour, and
I'll pay the rent ; but it would not answer me to
pay without it."   Nally has been duly served with
a writ—the services of a hundred constabulary

being necessary to protect the process server on that occasion, and under that compulsion Nally has paid ; so Mr. O'Hara hopes that ultimately the other tenants may follow his example. But while they hold aloof, fiom all sides come pouring in pressing demands for money. The interest and premiums on insurances were paid with the rent received; but the butcher is getting clamorous, the patience of the baker is nearly exhausted, and in the near future Mr. O'Hara sees no outcome from the strained relations between him and the tenants but payment, or eviction, with a protection post of constabulary quartered in Garrauns Castle.

CHAPTER XIV.

A DISPENSARY DOCTOR.

THE dispensary district of Belgorman was stirred to its very depths by the contest for the appointment vacant by the death of the dispensary doctor. The necessary advertisement for a successor was answered by forty-five applicants; and if the printed testimonials forwarded by each as to his industry, cleverness, promise as an ornament to the profession, and peculiar fitness for the vacant situation were to be depended upon, the medical profession was that year enriched by the addition of forty-five men whose early promise bespoke a genius and devotion to science that must one day shed a lustre upon the profession whose teachers so generously crowned them in anticipation.

Of the forty-five candidates but fifteen went so far as to canvass the members of the dispensary committee; and a fortnight before the election the field had dwindled down to two competitors, between whom the committee was so evenly divided that excitement was at fever point. Dr. McNamara was supported by all the influence of his father and the parish priest. His father, who was the proprietor of the principal shop in Belgorman, had many friends among the rural guardians; and Father Gavin left no stone unturned to show the impropriety and indecency of electing any but a Catholic doctor to attend to the health of a Catholic population. Guardians were warned that their voting for a Protestant would be an insult to the people; and to the people it was broadly insinuated that the new-fangled anxiety to appoint a Protestant doctor was in pursuance of a scheme certainly to mark the slavery of the people, and possibly to facilitate their extermination.

With so effectual a spur to excitement it was not surprising that the people of the Belgorman dispensary district were moved. For Mr. Townsend, a magistrate and owner of property in the neighbourhood, had adopted a Protestant candidate and connection, Dr. King, whose testimonials seemed equally satisfactory as the credentials of the other forty-four seekers. The committee in whose hands the election rested was composed of all the elected guardians for the divisions of which the dispensary district was formed, and all the magistrates qualified by property within the district to act as *ex-officio* guardians.

As the day approached the excitement waxed more intense, and it was considered prudent to secure the services of one hundred additional con-

stables for that day. At the last election, twelve
years before, Mr. Townsend took but little interest
in the matter, and voted for the person who had
secured the interest of Father Gavin. But at that
time the Irish Church had not been disestablished,
and except for the gratification of the parson's
vanity it mattered little the number of Protestants
in the parish. Now that a moiety of the parson's
stipend must be made up by the parochial subscriptions, Mr. Townsend felt a keen interest in
securing the presence of an additional paying
Protestant—an interest shared by every member
of the congregation.

The day of the election arrived, and from all the
country round hundreds of people poured into
Belgorman. Mr. Furlong, a Catholic gentleman
who deserted his faith for his order, and promised
his vote to his young friend Dr. King, was so
furiously stoned as he drove into the little town
that the constabulary were obliged to fix swords
and charge the people to enable him to get to the
committee room. As each Catholic guardian came
in he was cheered to the echo, while the Protestants and supporters of Dr. King had a bad
time of it. At length the decision was announced,
the numbers being—for Dr. King, 9; for Dr.
McNamara, 11. And the cheering was as loud as
if the announcement had been the grant of Home
Rule.

That was some years ago, and the youthful

L

enthusiasm with which Dr. McNamara began the practice of medicine has long since disappeared. He would no longer object to the services of old Betty Jennings as vicarious patient for the village of Pollnagreena. Betty was one of his first patients at the district dispensary. She described to him accurately her symptoms, which he treated by a prescription for lumbago. The next day she was there, suffering from what must be acute bronchitis, though he could not detect any evidence of the miseries she described with so much feeling. However, a bottle of cough mixture satisfied her. The following week she again appeared, and was warned to go home at once and go to bed, taking a mixture that Dr. McNamara hoped would bring out fully a rash that she assured him had appeared on her breast and back (which she declined to expose), and which from her description seemed like measles. An application next week for a prescription for the ague brought about an explanation. The village of Pollnagreena was almost entirely Irish-speaking; and, as a simple escape from the difficulty attending the diagnosis of their complaints by a doctor who did not understand Irish, the inhabitants delegated the old woman to describe the ailment from which they suffered, and thus procure medicine which they took without a question.

The district of Belgorman is a large one, and as every guardian and the clergy of each denomina-

tion, who are usually appointed as wardens, can
give a "red ticket" or order to the doctor to attend
forthwith at the house of any person entitled to
medical attendance, the doctor has from time to
time had hard work. The poor are fanciful in
their ailments ; and Dr. McNamara has more than
once found a person, to whose house he has driven
twelve or fourteen miles over rough by-roads on an
urgent order, sitting comfortably at dinner, the
ailment having subsided. He ought not to have
given tartar-emetic to Paddy Ellison for a tooth-
ache ; but his annoyance was so great at having to
drive six miles, and walk across a wet bog on a
stormy evening for three miles farther, in answer
to a message that Ellison's life was in danger, that
on finding the worthy only suffering from tooth-
ache he relieved his mind by a prescription that
effectually punished Ellison for his laziness in not
having gone to the doctor for relief. Now experience has hardened his heart, and many a poor
wretch tosses impatiently on his miserable bed for
many long hours after the time when the doctor
ought to have arrived.

More than once or twice complaints were made
to the board of guardians, but the explanation
given to the dispensary committee was always
considered satisfactory. Outside his connection
with many members of the committee, the
Catholic portion of that body would think twice
before they opened the situation to another con-

test. So the doctor is practically safe from everything short of a sealed order of dismissal despatched from the Local Government Board. One person he takes care never to offend. Father Gavin, who was so deeply interested in his success at the election, insists on his unquestioning obedience; and Father Gavin is too bitter an opponent not to be obeyed. Dr. McNamara was dissatisfied when the priest gave a red ticket to John Ratigan, who could well have afforded to pay him the usual fee. But he did not dare to refuse to visit Ratigan, who, in common with numbers of his well-to-do neighbours, thus obtains from time to time gratuitous attendance and medicine. When a visiting ticket cannot be secured, they prefer paying a fee to the bone-setter and general quack of the neighbourhood to calling in the doctor. After a fair the bone-setter has considerable practice in patching up broken heads; and the doctor is anxiously watching for a death under this practitioner's hands, that a verdict may possibly be obtained against him at the coroner's inquest.

The bone-setter's treatment is simple. The scalp wounds are generally severe when his aid is required, so he makes a preliminary examination by probing, during which he inserts a small piece of bone into the jagged wound, and, removing it before the admiring family, declares the skull is chipped but he will yet save the patient. Unsalted butter is then melted and poured into the wound, and a light plug of tow inserted. In the fulness of time the wound heals, and the bone-setter's fee is all the more gladly paid that his practice is illegitimate.

Dr. McNamara is married to the daughter of a wealthy farmer living in the district, whose influence on the committee would be of great assistance to his son-in-law should any evil befall him. When the investigation was held in consequence of the serious mischief done to Mrs. Scott by a mistake made while the doctor was drunk, his father-in-law stood by him, declaring that the doctor had left his house to attend to Mrs. Scott, and was perfectly sober ; which was, to say the least, not true : but it carried him through.

Dr. McNamara is in comfortable circumstances. His dispensary salary is £120. For each vaccination he receives 2*s.*, which brings in about £40 more ; a like amount per month for each policeman in the district adds another £40. As sanitary officer he has £10, and the registration of births brings in £20, giving him a settled income of £230 besides his private practice. Belgorman being a fighting neighbourhood, Dr. McNamara's " chances " may be set down at £80 more. When Peter Hunt, who had been beaten, called in the doctor, and, burning with desire for revenge, swore an information on which John Keating and Michael Carrol were arrested, Dr. McNamara handed in a certificate that Hunt's life was in danger. The magistrate thereupon refused to accept bail ; but next day, the pri-

soner's friends having paid the doctor four guineas,
a certificate was given that Hunt was now out of danger, upon which bail was accepted. Dr. McNamara
explains that, Hunt having received some scalp
wounds, erysipelas might have set in. Therefore
his life was in danger. Next day, on consideration,
he thought the patient's symptoms so favourable
that danger was no longer to be apprehended. The
case was of course prosecuted by Government, and
the doctor's fees for attendance at petty sessions
and quarter sessions amounted to eight guineas.
He thus made twelve guineas out of that case,
besides his fee for attendance upon Hunt; and
many similar cases may be annually counted upon.

Dr. McNamara's private practice is mainly confined to the farmers, as the gentry prefer the services
of the doctor in the next town, who has no dispensary. The practice of medicine among the farmers
and working people is so different to that among the
better classes, that a dispensary doctor must forget
his ordinary experience when treating people whose
nervous systems are so much more highly strung
and their digestive organs so much more delicate.
The poor people who sit round the door of the dispensary every week to take their turn for treatment
have not now much faith in Dr. McNamara: which
is not to be wondered at, as he boasts that he can
"polish off" thirty cases in as many minutes.
When Ellen Nulty was suffering from acute rheu-
matism, Father Gavin advised her to allow him to

send Dr. McNamara to see her; but she said she would rather die a natural death, and induced her husband to call in the quack. This longing for irregular attendance shows itself in many ways. Gratuitous vaccination is offered to the people; and though it is often practically useless—the vaccination being carelessly performed, and the lymph so deteriorated by transmission through large numbers of children of all kinds of constitutions—so far as the people know, it is quite efficacious. Yet nothing but compulsion brings the mothers to the dispensary, and more than one outbreak of small-pox has been traced by Dr. McNamara to the illegal inoculation of children. Judy Kirwan was prosecuted, but acquitted. She had her child inoculated in the usual manner. When the old woman who acted as operator came round, the child was left on the roadside with half a crown beside it. The mother retired for ten minutes, and on her return the child was inoculated and the half-crown had disappeared. Judy Kirwan's mother took small-pox from the child, and died; but even that catastrophe will not prevent Judy from leaving her next child under similar precautions against legal evidence of the criminal operation.

Dr. McNamara reads but little: he is a farmer, and all his spare time is given to the business of the farm. His medical knowledge remains pretty much what it was when he left the schools, his anatomical studies being continued at intervals by post-mortem examinations, made by direction of the coroners' juries on victims of violence. But of the advance of the science of his profession he is profoundly ignorant. New instruments are unknown—new prescriptions undreamt of. A rough knowledge of the treatment in ordinary cases is sufficient for his practice, and he has no ambition to do more than get comfortably through the year. One form of disease Dr. McNamara never attempts to cure—epilepsy. He gravely and seriously holds this to be a subject for exorcism rather than medicine, and recommends an appeal to Father Gavin, only directing that no pork or bacon be eaten ; for, since the misfortune to the herd of swine, the flesh of pigs is sure, if used, to bring on an attack from the evil spirit whose presence takes the form of epilepsy. Dr. McNamara has seen so many real cures performed by amulets, blessed threads of linen dipped in King Charles's blood, and other vehicles for the curative excitement of nerve-centres by the action of the will, that he is a firm believer in the supernatural.

The sanitation of the filthy little town of Belgorman could not be worse ; and when fever seizes on the place it is always difficult to get rid of it ; but nothing is farther from Dr. McNamara's mind than to earn his yearly £10 by really looking for nuisances with a view to their abatement, and thus bringing a hornets' nest about his ears. The dirtiest and most dangerous yard in the town belongs to a member of the dispensary committee, and others nearly as bad are owned by men who could bring influence to bear against him. He dare not excite the displeasure of his constituents by the performance of his duty ; nor is it expected that a man not appointed by Government should perform a duty that might make him unpopular Dr. Mc-Namara will continue to pay his dues to Father Gavin and abstain from giving offence to his committee ; and if he lives long enough to see his son duly enrolled in the medical profession, he will probably one day retire upon a pension, first securing the election of the rising genius as his successor in the dispensary district of Belgorman.

CHAPTER XV.

THE VOTER OF THE FUTURE.

IF the town of Drumgoole were more compact in its formation it would look like the dirt-heap of the plain in which it is situated. Its five hundred and fifty thatched cabins, that have attached themselves to the one hundred slated houses forming the town proper, straggle along the five converging roads that meet at the market-cross, where stands a pretentious town hall, whose unrepaired windows, broken by missiles flung by playful urchins, afford a genial example of disregard for appearances by the town council that is followed by the inhabitants with the frank *bonhomie* of the Irish nature.

For Drumgoole is governed by a town council, whose election, being strictly non-political, is a matter of so little interest that no change was ever known to take place in the representation save by the death of one of its members. The tolls and customs of the extensive market supply a fund sufficient to make the municipal arrangements perfect. But, except that from time to time a feeble effort is made to reset a loose flag on the footpath, the town council is careful to make no boastful appearance of spending the funds at its disposal. A contract is gravely entered into that the streets are to be kept clean, and occasionally the aged contractor is seen sounding with a scraper the depth of mud, until when two or three inches deep it seems worth while to collect it in heaps at the sides of the street. Farther than that he never moves it; yet it disappears like magic, and the mystery is only solved in spring, when from the hall doors emerge women bending under loads of manure, carried in baskets from the heaps in the back yards which have been accumulating for the past year. The evil-smelling mass, in which is a share of the valuable road-scrapings, is deposited in the street, and left for removal to the farms.

At this time it is not well to visit Drumgoole, which presents the appearance as if every house had turned right-about-face, at the same time stirring up its manure-heap for the benefit of the public. In Drumgoole the business of life is done in the face of the people. The bootmaker sits at his last, inside the door, and has not yet turned his shop into a " boot and shoe emporium." The tailor can answer inquiries from the front door, without leaving the board where he sits cross-legged, surrounded by his journeymen. The bare arms of the kneading baker can be seen at work as you drive past his house. The butcher points with pride to the carcass of a cow killed, skinned, and hung in the room where he and his family eat and sometimes sleep; or asks you to order a leg of the sheep tied and bound at the door of the "shop," into whose throat he plunges the knife, while a crowd of urchins stand around, taking early lessons in cruelty from the unpitying victualler.

These are the incidents of the town proper—the body of the starfish that it resembles in shape. Along the diverging limbs cabin has been added to cabin, until they stretch for half a mile in every direction. The detail of these houses is simple, four walls and a roof being the limit of architectural pretensions. As no land is attached except a small "garden" behind, the dimensions of the familiar dungpit are attenuated, and the live stock is represented by a few hens, which fly in and out over the half-door. The floors of the smoke-grimed cabins are dry, and, on the whole, though filthy to the last degree, they are almost as comfortable as an Indian wigwam.

In one of these cabins Denis Hogan has lived since his marriage, which was solemnized when he was twenty-three, as after that age a single man becomes talked about; and even among labourers old bachelordom is a reproach that must be avoided at all hazards, the contempt of the neighbours being added to the displeasure of the clergy. His provision for the union was a house, a table, two chairs, and a bedstead ; to which his bride added a feather-bed, the materials of which she had collected with much care for some years. Their worldly wealth besides was £2, half of which was paid to the priest as a fee ; and the morning following the wedding Hogan took his place as usual at the market-cross at half-past five, spade in hand, waiting, with a crowd of the neighbours, for his chance of employment that day.   Hogan's father and his grandfather were labourers, living in the same range of cabins, and the neighbours are also hereditary sons of daily toil.   Their ranks are rarely recruited from the sons of farmers, who, if they cannot obtain a share of the father's holding, generally emigrate to America rather than subside into a class that even the poorest farmer considers so much beneath him.

Hogan's family is no exception to the law of productiveness in proportion to approximation to the primitive state.   Each year has brought its increase ; the advent of twins on two occasions im- posing an undue strain upon the family resources. Fortunately, these oft-recurring events, which in other classes occasion so much anxiety, do not appear to interfere with Mrs. Hogan's comfort farther than the necessity for increased supervision for a time over the young brood.   Sometimes, even her day's work is not stopped for more than an hour or two, and before a fortnight the care of the latest arrival is handed over to Mary, the eldest

daughter at home, who numbers eleven summers
Here, a celibate clergy prevents the assistance that
at such times poor women receive in English
parishes, where the parson's wife does full share of
parochial work in providing the loan of necessaries
on co-operative principles. Did the wife of the
parson of Drumgoole dare to interfere with the
Catholic population, she would kindle a flame that
would soon make the town too hot to hold her.

Mrs. Hogan has been educated at the National
school, and can read and write. She even began to
learn a treatise upon Greek roots. But of sewing
or knitting or the most elementary principles of
cooking she is profoundly ignorant, as she is
oblivious of any idea of cleanliness. If she knew
anything of cooking, she might, even with the oatmeal, potatoes, cabbage, herrings, grease, and milk
which form the staple substances on which the
family live, make such a variety in their daily food
as would render it palatable. But the oatmeal is
always made into stirabout, the potatoes are boiled
in their skins, the cabbage coarsely dressed, and
the herrings fried.

Her children are clothed from the remnants of
her tattered garments. An old red flannel petticoat makes two frocks with long skirts, that are
worn indiscriminately by boys and girls, until at
nine or ten the boys are put into trousers. Her
Sunday dress, of a cheap but brilliant purple
material, was made by a neighbouring dress-

maker ; and even the home-made flannel petticoat, the materials of which she dyed herself with cutbear, was shaped by the dressmaker before she sewed it roughly together. Of knitting she does not feel the want, as except a pair of cotton stockings for Sunday, worn when the purple dress is donned, no member of the family wears boots or socks, save her husband, who could not otherwise do his spade-work properly.

When Hogan is out of work Mrs. Hogan sees no shame in a little begging, but rather glories in a poverty that she believes, in common with most of her faith, must ensure to her the kingdom of heaven in the future in compensation for her position on earth as one of "the Lord's poor." Besides, if the practice of charity be necessary to salvation, there must be recipients as well as donors ; and in asking for alms Mrs. Hogan feels that she is only performing her part in a partnership of faith, in which the benefits from the transaction are equally divided. There can be, therefore, no degradation in supplying a necessary outlet for a necessary stream. Nor does she ignore the danger to the soul of refusal ; and the beggar who asks at her door for a potato never leaves without one being added to his sack if there are any in the house.

In the spring and autumn Mrs. Hogan shares with her husband the regular labour. She can cut the potatoes for seed, or lay the seed that is to be covered by the men. She too, with other women, spreads the manure, carrying it from the heap deposited by the carts, in a basket which, having filled on the heap, she carries on her back to the ridge and spreads in her hands. She receives but half a man's wages, whether weeding, spreading, binding corn, or turning hay, but performs fully a man's share of the labour. All the money earned by the family is in her possession, and her husband rarely trenches upon the provision for the idle seasons except when he indulges in a visit to the public-house.

Every Monday the clothes not required for use on week-days are placed in the pawn office, not more for the money thus set free, than because there they are safely stowed until Saturday, when they are duly released for Sunday's wear. Mrs. Hogan's eldest daughter has at last procured a place as housemaid in a gentleman's house. She began as maid-of-all-work in a public-house in Drumgoole, and changed to better places, until, hearing of the situation at Mrs. Jameson's, she was fortunate enough to obtain it. Mrs. Jameson was anxious to get a farmer's daughter to come to her; but no farmer's daughter would demean herself by going to service—marriage, a teachership of a National school, or employment as shop-girls, being the objects of their ambition. Domestic servants must therefore be drawn from the labourers, and Ellen Hogan is a very honest girl. Mrs. Jameson complains of her want of cleanliness; but if she could see the cabin in which Ellen was brought up she might understand how difficult it must be to forget the lessons of the most impressionable part of a life, and learn in a few years to eradicate the familiarity with squalor which cannot see that dirt on floor or table is matter in the wrong place.

Denis Hogan's life is not eventful. At half-past five o'clock in summer and half-past six in winter he is found at the market-cross, armed with a spade, a scythe, or a pitchfork, as the case may be, and looking for employment for the day. Sometimes he is fortunate enough to obtain regular work for a week or fortnight from a farmer, and two or three times he was employed during the hurried season at Mr. Gardiner's farm.

This is the blue riband of the labour of Drumgoole. Here the labourer fortunate enough to be enrolled on the regular list has constant work at ten shillings a week. Mr. Gardiner always provides labour for the staff of workmen. On wet days they find something to be done indoors, and thus no half-days are made for broken weather. The farmers make much harder bargains. No farmer will give more than one shilling a day for constant labour; and though those who are not thus employed get as much as two shillings a day in the busy seasons, they cannot get more than tenpence when the hurried time has passed. A day's labour, too, under the eye of a steward and in the company of a farmer are two very different things,

M

the latter extracting ten per cent. more work, and carefully deducting the broken time.

Denis Hogan then does not love the farmers, while in the gentlemen he sees men who in their relations have treated him fairly. His politics are of a negative type, and though he does not dare to say that the parish priest is wrong in declaring that the tyranny of landlordism is unbearable, he knows to his cost the difference in the treatment of labourers by the landlords and the farmers. His house, for which he pays a shilling a week, belongs to a farmer who served him with notice to quit in the summer of 1879 because three weeks' rent was due, when at the time the same farmer refused to pay the landlord his rent, one year in arrear, except at an abatement of 25 per cent.

Hogan heard at the next anti-rent meeting the vengeance of Heaven called down upon the land-lord's head for his treatment of the farmer in refusing the abatement, but was too shy to say before so many how sternly the down-trodden farmer insisted upon the punctual satisfaction of his own claims to the bitter end. He attended the meeting, as did all the neighbours, for the excitement of seeing the crowd with the green banners and sashes, tin pikes, mock guns, and array of horsemen robbing the patient plough-horses of their fairly earned Sunday's rest. With the political aspect of the Sunday's gathering he has no concern, and merely goes to see the sights and hear the speaking, being by nature as fond of oratory as an Athenian. When his day's work is over he is too glad of the rest from physical weariness to trouble himself about political conspiracies. Nor are the ranks of discontent generally swelled by men whose days are passed in active toil. The blacksmith and carpenter are men of weight in the town. The shoemakers and tailors join the wilder spirits among the shopmen in working out impossible schemes of political salvation, and supply the mental activity that makes the recurring little conspiracies troublesome.

Denis Hogan has no hope of ever being in possession of one acre of land, and the land agitation has therefore for him but little practical interest. To a certain extent, indeed, he does farm every year. In spring he takes a quarter of an acre in conacre from some farmer near the town who is letting land for potatoes preparatory to taking an oat crop off it next year. The land is taken for the crop by various labouring men, who are only charged the rent paid by the farmer on condition that they manure it. The farmer has thus his land manured for the next year's oat crop for nothing. Hogan tills a quarter of an acre every year, and the potatoes usually last to the next spring. He tried sowing a crop of oats in conacre one year, but the rent of soil for an oat crop being £8 an acre he made nothing by it.

Hogan is singularly insensible to beauty of form

or colour. The golden tints of the setting sun upon the purple mountains that form the sky-line from Drumgoole have for him no beauty. The little river stealing by its grassy banks flecked with daisies and buttercups never tempts him to sit and watch its course. The dog-violets and primroses that challenge admiration as they brighten the roadside fences with patches of brilliant colour he passes unheeding by.

> "A primrose by the river's brim
> A yellow primrose was to him,
> And it was nothing more."

Even woman's beauty has for him but little charm, and in arranging the marriage with his wife he was influenced by her size and strength of body and constitution rather than by any personal attractions she might have possessed.

Hogan's brother served in the army, and his tales of foreign parts have inspired Jemmy Hogan with a longing to enlist. This resolve is a great grief to Mrs. Hogan, who has a very poor opinion of the army, and would much prefer her son's seeking work in England when he is old enough to accompany the harvestmen who go over every year. Still the pensioner points to his pension for life, and shows that when sickness or old age overtakes him he can live in the free air of heaven, instead of feeling that his days may possibly be ended in the poorhouse, which the presence of eternal whitewash and the absence of tobacco render miserable in the extreme.

Hogan cannot be called a drunkard. From time to time he indulges in two or three glasses of whisky or porter, on which occasions he generally falls into the hands of the police and is duly fined. But as a rule he is abstemious, and only drinks now and again to procure excitement—almost the only kind that he experiences in the dull monotony of his existence. He is mightily fond of a game of cards, and often stakes his penny with six or seven others in a game of " five and twenty," when if the five, knave, or ace of hearts stand his friend he may win the price of half a day's labour. This is his only relaxation. Dances have practically ceased, so he cannot have the pleasure of even looking on. Hurling matches are no more. Wakes come but seldom. Coffee-houses are unknown. Now and again a bout of drinking with a friend makes his blood course freely through his veins. The stream of Lethe flows through the public-house tap, and excitement is followed by oblivion, where he forgets for a time that hardship and squalor and uncertainty for the future are his, and toil and labour go on for ever.

CHAPTER XVI.

A NATIONAL SCHOOLMASTER.

WHEN Mr. Dixon was induced to build a National schoolhouse on his property he did so in the most economical manner. Close by an unoccupied house, which was allotted to the schoolmaster, a plain slated building was erected, of which the single room afforded accommodation for one hundred scholars. No ornamentation of any kind was permitted to swell the modest estimate of the architect; for Mr. Dixon is a utilitarian, and has a rooted objection to what he calls architectural fal-lals. However, having built the school and undertaken to pay half the teacher's salary, he determined to obtain for his people the best schoolmaster he could get, and for that purpose he applied to the model training college in Dublin, where, under the direction of the Commissioners of Education, men and women are specially trained, and receive certificates of qualification for the situation of National schoolmasters and schoolmistresses. In due course a schoolmaster was appointed who held a first-class certificate; school requisites were provided, and around the walls hung maps of different countries, pictures of birds and beasts, and diagrams of various mechanical combinations—wheel, lever, rack, and pinion, inclined plane, and the rest.

But in taking upon himself the appointment of a schoolmaster Mr. Dixon counted without his host. So far as building the schoolhouse, and guaranteeing half the teacher's salary, his action was entirely commendable; but in appointing a schoolmaster he had overlooked the necessity of consulting the parish priest, who lost no time in showing him the result of such an attempt to throw over the spiritual pastor. Father Johnston called upon Mr. Dixon and explained to him that the secular principles of the Government training establishment were denounced by the hierarchy, and however such a system might be approved of by the Education Commissioners he would not allow the children of his flock to be tainted by secularism in education. Mr. Dixon refused to reconsider the appointment made by him as patron and manager; and the consequence was that for twelve months the master of Kinveagh National School had an easy time of it, not one of the children attending the school, while all of them marched past the door to another school five miles away. Ultimately Mr. Dixon bowed to the inevitable, and dispensed with the services of the trained teacher, who was in the mean time deprived of the rights of the Church by

Father Johnston, and obliged at intervals to go by rail to a distant city for the spiritual consolations of which he felt in need.

Having given way, Mr. Dixon surrendered at discretion, and the next appointment was made on Father Johnston's recommendation. James Farrel had never had any special training as a teacher, except that when he was a boy he had assisted as a monitor in teaching a class in the National school at which he was educated. Still he was a clever young man, and in a little while passed successfully the test examination to which he was subjected by the inspector of National schools before his appointment could be confirmed. He has in time succeeded in passing through three grades, and is now a second-class teacher receiving a salary of £38 a year, besides his allowances such as result-fees and school charges. To attain this position he has been obliged to pass in spelling, grammar, geography, school organization, lesson-books and money matters, methods of teaching, arithmetic, geometry and mensuration, algebra, natural philosophy, mechanics, book-keeping, and agriculture.

Farrel is, then, a fairly educated man, and possesses no small influence in the neighbourhood. His neighbours consult him as to the correctness of their market accounts, when, puzzled by fractions, they fear that they may have been cheated by the buyers. Agreements as to division of farms, or arrangements before marriage, are generally pre-

pared by him; and the fact that a trifling in-
accuracy in Mrs. Nelligan's will carried the bulk of
that worthy woman's property to the wrong person
has not deposed him from his position as the principal drawer of wills in the Kinveagh school district.

At ten every morning the school wakes up to its
daily duties. As the children drop in by groups
they give their names to the master, and each
urchin deposits in winter his contribution of one
or two sods of turf on the heap formed to supply
a fire in the schoolroom for the general comfort.
Kinveagh is not a populous district, and the average
attendance at the school represents a large proportion of the children within its bounds. Even
labourers readily pay when they can the penny a
week demanded from them, while the better-to-do
people pay double that amount. Around the walls
are the various maps before mentioned, and behind
the master's chair are hung the four sheets containing the rules and regulations of the Commissioners
of National Education. Of course no pupil has
ever had the audacity to read these rules, nor does
Farrel think it quite consistent with the dignity of
his position that the parents of the pupils should
consider him bound by any regulations in his mode
of instruction. The Scripture lesson on toleration
—the love of our enemies and consideration for
those whose opinions differ from our own—displayed
on the second sheet, the principles of which the
Commissioners require to be strictly inculcated,

Farrel thinks poor stuff, the teaching of which rather tends to hamper the power of faith and take the backbone out of true religious fervour. If, he argues, we are weakly to tolerate a false religion, what is to be said of those who in times gone by have struck a blow for the true faith ? So he exercises his discretion by ignoring as far as possible the Scripture lesson. Nor does it seem necessary for the comfort of the school that lessons in toleration should be daily inculcated ; for it does not contain a single Protestant.

Three times a year Kinveagh is visited by the district inspector, who examines the children and notes their proficiency in various subjects. On their answering depends Farrel's result-fees, and the preparation for the approaching visit is an anxious time for him. Nor is the examination a mere repetition of the lessons which the children have already gone through, questions being put to them to test the amount of knowledge which they have really acquired. "What is success ?" asked the inspector, interrupting Tommy Murphy in his reading ; and Tommy's answer, "Good luck, sir," was nearer to the truth than the more elaborate explanation in Sullivan's Spelling-book.

Outside the inspector's visits Farrel is practically free from supervision. Mr. Dixon has not come near the school since his appointment, and Father Johnston's visits can hardly be called a check upon his proceedings. His salary is a fixed amount, and his result-fees and capitation grant are but slightly varying sums. Once, indeed, he was in trepidation for a time. An anxious lady whose property supplied nearly half the Kinveagh pupils was induced by the priest of the adjoining parish to offer it a schoolhouse and a guarantee for the master's salary, and the matter seemed all but arranged. Farrel was in very low spirits about it, but fortunately for him the project fell through. About a week after Mrs. Sinclair had consented to build the schoolhouse the parish priest called upon her to say that the bishop disapproved of schools of which the patronage was not vested in the clergy. Mrs. Sinclair answered that practically he would be the patron, as she did not intend to take any active part in the management of the school ; but, as she was to build it and pay half the teacher's salary, she could not consent to resign the patronage into other hands. She was then informed that in that case she might establish the school if she liked, but no Catholic child should attend it.

Master of his own actions and beyond the moulding influences of departmental discipline, Farrel's principles are profoundly affected by the prevailing mode of thought of the neighbourhood, which is decidedly antagonistic to existing social arrangements. Yet, as the life of a teacher is the experience of a little despot, he expects that his social and political convictions shall be received with unquestioning acquiescence. Therefore when he joined the brotherhood who have taken into their hands the control of the relations between landlord and tenant, he did so as an adviser, who is to be consulted in all cases of difficulty. Although half Farrel's fixed salary is paid by the public he in no sense considers himself a servant of the State, and his mental attitude towards the Government is precisely the same as that of the surrounding farmers. The person by whom he is appointed, paid, and may be dismissed is the patron ; and until the time draws near when he may look forward to the receipt of a pension he has no communication with any public department.

The regulations order that not only is he to inculcate loyalty, but he is to refrain from taking part in any political demonstrations. But such instructions are liberally interpreted, and unfortunately Farrel's loyalty is not in the direction contemplated by the framers of the regulation. In 1867 he was regarded by the police with grave suspicion, and he declares that his brother, who is a constable, is no better than a traitor to his country. Again, when Mr. Enright, who had purchased a small property in the Landed Estates Court, began to improve his investment by the addition of 45 per cent. to the rental, and immediately received two or three threatening letters requesting him to prepare his coffin, Farrel's handwriting was made the subject of careful investigation. On both occasions surmise was insufficiently confirmed, and he escaped a prosecution. Farrel is a doctrinaire, drawing his inspiration from the colums of the *Shamrock*, the *Flag of Ireland*, and the *Irish World*. An indefatigable reader, he daily consults the *Freeman's Journal*. But such constitutional pabulum is only accepted pending the weekly issue of the more advanced exponents of Irish opinion.

The journal on which Farrel pins his political faith is the *Irish World*, the circulation of which he endeavours to increase by recommendations to his friends. Seated by Murty Gleeson's fire, he reads to an attentive audience the contents of that organ of American Socialism, and sighs for the day when landlords and capitalists shall be no more. Fenianism is dormant, and Farrel's friends no longer look for autonomy in which the present social fabric is to remain intact. Farrel is prepared to accept the most extreme propositions concerning land, labour, capital, and interest in the Communistic creed. Still, great as may be the dignity of labour, he does not intend that his son shall be a tradesman, or even a National school teacher. When he has attained the proper age he will enter into competition for the Civil Service, and with every prospect of success, too; while his father looks forward to the cultivation of a little farm, which, with his pension of £30 a year, will be sufficient to support him. He has not yet begun to think over the probability of finding a little farm vacant, and does not see that the principles of

which he approves will, if successful, render it all
the more difficult for an outsider to obtain a farm
at all, be it little or big.

Farrel is animated by a real love for his country,
and is so far a true patriot.   Unfortunately his
honest attachment to Ireland is fed by theories
unsubstantial as soap-bubbles, and these theories
are but too likely to be for the present imbibed by
the youth committed to his charge.   Blinded by
the demand for an equality which has no existence
in nature, and unballasted by the possession of
even one acre of land, he presents a political problem the solution of which can only be hoped for
by the exercise of patience, generosity, and good
temper.

CHAPTER XVII.

A "GOMBEEN" MAN.

MUCH abused as is James Foley, many of his neighbours know that but for his timely assistance when the landlord's rent or the shopkeeper's demand had to be met they would have been obliged to pay costs, and perhaps have suffered the horrors of eviction. James Foley has been a money-lender for many years. He began his career on returning from a successful migration to England, when a neighbour who required ten pounds offered to give him two pounds for the loan of that amount for six months. From that moment the die was cast, and, the sweets of discount once tasted, he turned his money month by month, spending nothing except what sufficed for his bare necessities, and working hard to add to his store, until at length he found himself in possession of a goodly sum and settled in a small farm—most of his labour being done as complimentary work by his numerous debtors and those who wished to stand well with the gombeen man in view of possible contingencies. The derivation of the word "gombeen" is obscure. The termination "een" is the diminutive in Irish—"potteen" signifying a little pot, "bohereen" a little road, "cruiskeen" a little jar. "Gombeen" means a money-lender; but "gom" means a fool, and the annals of usury will hardly justify the use of the diminutive in addition as the proper equivalent for a bill-discounter.

The discount charged by Foley is generally about 30 per cent., or 1s. 6d. in the pound for three months. Of course this is for well-assured sums, where the promissory note is given by two or three joint securities ; but when more risky business is done the discount increases, until for small amounts, as much as cent. per cent. has been paid in kind.

Not even the parish priest knows more family secrets than does James Foley. Among his best clients are the women, who barter in advance their eggs and butter for small loans to cover expenditure to which the husbands would strongly object. Half the produce of Biddy Brady's thirteen hens was duly handed over for an entire season in payment of the interest on a loan of £5, and Foley knew so well the average number of eggs that she could not cheat him of even six in a week. Biddy Brady does not like to tell her husband of that debt, for he is a respectable man and would disapprove of it highly. Indeed, his thrift was the cause of the drain going on in the income of the establishment ; for he refused to permit his wife to buy a new cloak on the ground that her present one was not quite worn out, and such stinginess could not be tolerated by any woman of spirit. She has almost exhausted her ingenuity in accounting for the way by which she purchased the cloak ; but the truth must come out one day, and then the cloak will be for a time a garment of sorrow.

Foley had established a large business before the National Bank opened a branch in the neighbouring town. Its advent at once deprived him of all the really solvent customers, who now borrowed at 10 per cent. the money for which they had hitherto paid thirty. But a large class still remains whose security is so doubtful that their credit is worthless. To men like these he still gives loans, watching his opportunity to obtain repayment. He rarely appeals to the law for the recovery of his money. So long as the people are allowed to pay by small instalments they honestly strive to pay their debts, and, the money yielding good interest, Foley is content to receive the smallest amount, the discount and premium being paid on the renewal. Though the establishment of a branch bank has deprived Foley of the most secure portion of his business, it has enabled him to increase his small loans tenfold. He is known in the bank as a solvent man, and the bills given to him are duly entered to his account ; and as the bank will renew

N

for him readily, he suffers no inconvenience from protracted payment.

Many stories are current in the neighbourhood as to the origin of Foley's wealth. As his father was but a labourer, and he began life in the same humble position, his friends cannot believe that he could have amassed his money by thrift, however self-denying, or industry, however unflagging. The rapid increase of capital by multiplication of small discounts is a mystery beyond their comprehension, and the attainment of wealth is by acclamation attributed to a fortunate meeting with a Leprehawn.

To the Celtic mind this supernatural good luck presents no feature of difficulty; for even Mr. Duffy, the schoolmaster, acknowledges the all-pervading presence of the various classes of fairies. Indeed, the matter admitted of no doubt, for ocular demonstration of their wicked interference was given when Mrs. Jackson's child gradually faded away without any apparent cause. Various charms were tried, but without avail ; and it was remarked that when the neighbours said "God bless him," and spat in his face for luck, he screamed, and displayed such symptoms of infantile ferocity as left no doubt that the fairies had succeeded in spiriting the real child away and leaving in its place one of themselves, who, in the dead of night, when no one was looking, changed from a pining infant into a withered crone, until the approach of some one

compelled it to resume the appearance of the
stolen child.

No one could quite account for the way in
which the ever-watchful fairies succeeded in obtaining possession of the child. Maybe it had sneezed
and no one said "God bless it," or yawned
three times while the mother was asleep, and thus
prevented from repeating the protective blessing.
The house-leek was growing on the house ; a cross
was on the door, a bottle of holy water hung at the
head of the bed, and every possible precaution
against fairies had been taken, no person in the
house ever venturing to speak of them except respectfully as the "good people." Anyhow, the
mischief was done, and in due course the substituted
child went through the form of dying, and was
buried with a feeling of relief.

There could be no doubt, then, in Killballyegan
of the existence of fairies ; and the secret of Foley's
good fortune was freely accepted. Killballyegan
contains many circular raths, and tumuli, which remains are the circular fences round the residences
of the ancient Celts, and the burial mounds beneath
which rest the bones of many a hardy warrior. But
the people know better. They know that out of the
old raths at twelve o'clock at night issue troops of
ladies and gentlemen in gorgeous costumes, with
horses and dogs. They have been seen to ride
races, and whole troops have disappeared into rath
or mound at full gallop as the early dawn was

ushered in by cock-crow. Of course no person would dare to be the first to desecrate a rath by turning a sod, for misfortune to him or his would surely follow.

One morning Foley walked out very early, and as he passed close to a rath he saw seated on a stone a little man about twelve inches high. He was dressed in a red coat covered with gold lace, and a cocked hat, and was so busily engaged in mending a shoe that he did not perceive Foley. Such an opportunity only presented itself to one in millions ; but Foley was not for a moment at fault. He knew that if he could catch the Leprehawn, and keep him, without taking his eyes off him for an instant, he would in the end be shown a crock of gold ; so, stealing lightly behind the sprite, he grasped him tightly, nor loosened his hold, though the shrill screams of the Leprehawn were heartrending. After many ineffectual devices on the part of the captive fairy to induce Foley to remove his gaze for an instant, at length he consented to show him the spot where the long-buried crock of gold was to be found, and from that day Foley was a rich man. The details of this story have been amplified, and Foley has often been appealed to for corroboration. However the story originated, Foley is better pleased that his success should be so explained, than that the people of Killballyegan should think he had become rich on the proceeds of their money.

Foley is a very regular attendant at fairs and markets. He may not have anything for sale, but he takes careful notes of the sales and purchases of his neighbours. He can tell to a lamb the stock in possession of every person around, and confounded Paddy Ellis, who refused his demand for the payment of an instalment on the ground that he handed over his oats to the landlord for rent, by telling him that he had the day before received five pounds fourteen for the oats in hard cash from a corn-dealer.

He sold all his litter of pigs on credit. The bargain was that ten shillings over the market price was to be paid by the purchaser; the money not to be paid until the pig had been re-sold. Tom Barry thought he did a good stroke of business when he fattened the pig and killed it for his own use, refusing to pay Foley. He defended the process for the amount, on the plea that as he had not re-sold the pig the time for payment had not come; but in this case ingenuity was not rewarded, for a decree was granted for the amount claimed.

A hard man is Foley, when his money is in danger, and fearless as a hero in the recovery of a doubtful debt. Yet at times he has been lavish in his expenditure. In his success, as in his poverty, family affection has remained green and vigorous, and when his father was dying he determined that he should have a respectable wake. The old man watched the preparations with the keenest interest, and as his peaceful end approached he noted with a quiet pleasure the completion of the brown pall, ornamented with white satin cross and bows, that was to cover him while the funeral festivities were in progress. Everything was made tidy, and the candles already lit before he breathed his last, and for three nights the neighbours flocked to the house to pay the last mark of respect to the deceased. Helping themselves to tobacco and snuff from plates laid upon the legs and breast of the dead parent, and to whisky, of which a plentiful supply was on the table, they sat round the room, chatting and singing songs, or playing some romping game to keep up the spirits of the family; and James Foley noted with pride the numbers that assembled next day to accompany the funeral.

Many attempts have been made by the farmers of Killballyegan to secure for a son-in-law so "warm" a man; but Foley feels that a wife would be a disturbing element in his business, and the cares of a money-lender are not conducive to the tender passion. He has therefore resisted all offers of alliance with his neighbours. Not even Betty Houlahan's £200 could tempt him; though at one time her parents fondly hoped that it would have been a match. Indeed, the affair was in a fair way to a satisfactory arrangement, for a mutual friend had visited Foley and told him that on the day of the marriage the £200 would be placed in his hands in hard cash. Foley was so far tempted that he promised to go over the following day and pay a visit to the Houlahans. Great preparations were made to receive him, and Betty Houlahan appeared in a silk dress, determined to display her charms to the greatest advantage. But here she made what a huntsman would call a wrong cast. Foley was to be tempted by money, not charms, and the silk dress settled the matter. He made a rapid survey of Betty's attire : that silk dress must have cost £6, and the kerchief fastened by a gorgeous brooch at least 10s. more. The boots were unfitted for field work, and the general get-up more suited to the shop than the farm. Foley calculated that it would take at least the interest of her money to satisfy her wants, and in such a marriage he could not see his way to any profit ; so the marriage fell through. He is now looked upon as a determined old bachelor ; and as he has no near relatives, a cousin "six o' kin," at present working as a farmer's boy, is looking forward to the time when he may step in for a valuable inheritance.

But Foley has no intention of leaving his money for the enrichment of his connections. He loves money for money's sake ; and if he could take it with him he would require no other heaven. But as he cannot, he at least may secure to himself hereafter some benefit from the hard work of accumulation in this world. He has determined to leave the greater portion of his money to be expended in masses for his soul, that his term of purgatory may thus be shortened ; and the direction in which the remainder may be left will greatly depend upon the views of the person who writes his tardy will, when, at the last, his wearied brain will escape from the trouble of decision by assenting to the proposals of the neighbour who has hurriedly been called upon to inscribe his last will and testament.

CHAPTER XVIII.

THE TRUE STORY OF THE IRISH FAMINE.

I.

As the time approaches for the winding up of the various funds formed for the relief of the Irish "Famine," it may not be without interest to consider the causes that led to these appeals and the manner in which the funds have been distributed. Bad as were the harvests in 1877–78, little was heard in Ireland of depression until the commercial failures in England compelled the Irish banks to contract their credits. Hitherto the banks had extended their business but too well. The shopkeepers followed suit, and the people, bitten by a system of reckless credit, entered upon a course of extravagance that could not last.

The inauguration of the anti-rent agitation found the people just beginning to feel the withdrawal of the ready accommodation to which they had become accustomed. The banks were then making considerable efforts to obtain payment of the outstanding

bills, and renewals were positively refused. Still
things were not desperate. The shopkeepers had
not yet refused to sell their goods on account ; and
while the baker and grocer continued the supplies,
the fact that the bank remained unpaid could be
borne ·with equanimity, for banks are slow to
institute legal proceedings.

So matters remained, until, in view of the approaching May rents, the wildest declarations of
povery and ruin were made from the platforms of
the anti-rent promoters and in the columns of the
press, until so effectually was the tenants' credit
cried down that the shopkeepers took them at
their word, and insisted upon a ready-money business for the present. At the same time some shopkeepers did a crafty stroke of business by joining
the anti-rent agitation, and proclaiming the im-
morality of paying the rent to the landlord until
after the shopkeepers' demands had been fully and
honestly met.

Matters thus went on during spring and summer.
Sunday after Sunday meetings were held at almost
every village in the west of Ireland, the language
being progressively intensified ; and, as the deluge
of August and September continued week after
week, the green oat crop looking as if it would never
ripen, the potatoes checked in their growth, and the
turf still lying on the bog as wet as when it was
cut in the spring, the cry of famine was repeated
at every meeting, and even wise men shook their

heads and wondered if the poor rates would bear what promised to be a tremendous pressure. So late as the 5th of June the Roman Catholic Archbishop of Tuam had written to the *Freeman's Journal* publicly denouncing the action of the knot of agitators that afterwards formed the nucleus of the Land League. But before the end of August the Roman Catholic priests had, with few exceptions, been irresistibly drawn into the movement, and were to be found on every platform, loud in denunciation of the present social system.

It was in September, while the summer rains still continued, that the inspectors of the Local Government Board visited their various districts. No wonder they reported that the potato crop would not give half its usual yield; that the general harvest was deficient in quantity and quality, and that the turf crop was practically lost. But with September the rain ceased, and before the official report was issued by the Local Government Board on the 28th of October the corn had already ripened, and yielded an average crop. The sodden turf would not have been saved by twenty-eight days of October fine weather; but, fortunately, from the 1st of October to the 1st of January we had but three days' rain, so that the wells showed symptoms of running dry. With such weather, it may well be accepted that the turf, though inferior, was by no means lost, and then the remainder of the winter was exceptionally fine.

So fine was it that the hay stored for the winter feeding of cattle was not required, and large quantities are even now (in June, 1880) being offered for sale at a low price. The potato crop was the one whose loss seemed most assured. While the potatoes were being dug, Commissioners went through the country making close inquiries as to the state of affairs. The reports were all the same : the crop was lost.

A couple of anecdotes may throw some light upon these reports. A gentleman, anxious to see for himself, walked into a field where the potatoes were being dug. He saw an excellent crop.

"I am glad," he said to the owner, "that you seem to have a good crop."

"Good crop, your honour! Not a basket of white potatoes you could get on a whole ridge," he answered, in apparent distress.

The gentleman, who was a practical farmer, said, "Well, I should like to get a basket of black potatoes, and I will give half a crown for a basket off this ridge."

"Begor, then, the money 'll soon be earned," said the owner, as he took a basket and walked along the ridge. He could not fill it, and returned saying, "Ah, sure, I wouldn't take your honour's money for bad potatoes." Then, seeing from some remark made by the gentleman that he lived in the country, he said, "Well, thanks be to God! they are not bad ; but sure I thought your honour was one of them English gentlemen that's going round."

I went into over one hundred potato fields in the west of Ireland, and saw the potatoes dug. In some the yield was excellent; in the majority a little more than the usual proportion of diseased tubers was apparent. In three fields the crop was practically lost. I always asked what the crop was like before I examined the potatoes. Invariably the answer was, "They are bad." One day I asked the usual question as I drove past a small field where a girl was busily engaged in carrying the potatoes to the potato pit.

" They are all bad, sir," was the answer.

I went in, and saw one of the finest crops I have ever seen. " Where are the black ones ? " I asked.

" Och, sure, there aren't many," she replied, quite unabashed.

" But I see none," I continued.

" Troth, they're fair enough," she said, laughing.

She had evidently taken me for a Commissioner.

One thing is certain. All through the winter potatoes sold in the western towns at from 4*d.* to 5*d.* per stone, and were to be bought in April at 6*d.*; and while shiploads of potatoes were being imported into Ireland, at least an equal quantity was being exported to Wales and England.

With such an allegation as convulsed the west of Ireland in the autumn, and with repeated statements that famine stared the people in the face, the collection of rent was no easy matter, however a landlord might see for himself that the farmers were not so badly off as they maintained. Mr. Parnell declared in his speech at Castlebar, in December, that his plan of refusing to pay a larger rent than the tenants considered fair would save them four millions of money. If the amount of rent still due be added to the abatements freely made by the Irish landlords, Mr. Parnell's estimate of the money granted by the landlord or appropriated by the tenant is not far wrong. All this time the shops were doing a good ready-money business, though the debts remained outstanding. The 150,000 people dependent upon the money earned by harvestmen, in England, were in great distress, and many were obliged to apply to the workhouse, as were some of the labourers. A few of the small farmers also felt the want of money.

Grazing farmers had lost very heavily from the ruinous fall of prices, but the tillage farmers were in by no means a bad way; while many landlords were obliged to shut up their houses and reduce their expenditure to suit their straitened circumstances.

On the 16th of December the Duchess of Marlborough made her appeal through the columns of the *Times*. Her Grace assumed that there would be extreme misery and suffering among the poor of the western counties and in the county of Cork, owing to loss of turf, loss of cattle, failure of potatoes, and want of employment. Her Grace prefaced this statement by the acknowledgment that the Government had already initiated certain measures for affording employment, and that in numerous cases the landlords were nobly standing by their people. Hitherto there were many people in Ireland who, while acknowledging severe pressure, could not find in any part of the country a state of affairs necessitating an appeal to the charity of the world. It was whispered that on Mr. Gray's accession to office he would inaugurate his mayoralty by an appeal to the public on behalf of the starving poor. Though Mr. Gray was in no sense a follower of Mr. Parnell, it is known that no Home Rule Irish member, whatever his private opinions, could refuse his sanction to a declaration of famine that went to accentuate the assertion of landlord tyranny in Ireland.

But with the wife of the Lord-Lieutenant it was very different. It was assumed that her Grace had official sanction for an appeal of so tremendous an import, and a ready response was given from almost every country in Europe. In due course an appeal was published from the Lord Mayor of Dublin, and the greater portion of money given for Irish distress has been subscribed through the Mansion House Fund. The Irish Land League followed suit, to a certain extent, and the *New York Herald* relief fund supplies the fourth stream by which the charitable donations of the world have been poured into Ireland. How these funds have been distributed in the west of Ireland will be seen in the next chapter.

II.

THE last chapter showed the state of affairs in Ireland up to the 16th of December, when the appeal was made by the Duchess of Marlborough. Besides the people dependent upon the harvest money earned in England there were a few circumscribed areas in the counties of Roscommon, Galway, and Donegal where great distress was to be apprehended ; for in these small districts the loss of the potato crop was much beyond the average. Her Grace's appeal was warmly responded to by the people of England, and subscriptions began to pour in. With the advent of the new Lord Mayor of Dublin a second appeal was made from the Mansion House, and a central committee formed of influential people representing every phase of opinion, religious and political. It may be stated at once that, so far as the central committees were concerned, the allocation of the funds placed at their disposal was as fair, and the plan of distribution as theoretically perfect, as ingenuity could devise for the disbursement of large charitable funds.

But a great scheme of charity is always a dangerous experiment, and in no country in Europe are its dangers more patent than in Ireland, not yet quite recovered from the demoralization resulting from the distribution of money after the famine of 1848. No sooner had it become apparent that the charitable world responded to the appeals

·set before it than preparations were made in every part of Ireland to secure a rivulet from the Pactolian stream, and a competition in mendicancy began, increasing in urgency of demand and extravagance of assertion to the present moment. Committees were formed in every county, one might almost say in every parish, and letters appeared daily in the papers, generally from the parish priest, saying that gaunt famine stared them in the face, and starvation, widespread and terrible, could only be prevented by immediate and generous assistance.

The markets were thronged with well-dressed people ; the shops were filled with customers ; the pawn-offices showed empty shelves, and sensible people read with astonishment that while Indian corn sold at $7\frac{1}{2}d.$ per stone, and potatoes, oats, eggs, and fowl filled the markets, the comfortable-looking people were starving. No appeals had been made to private houses, and the workhouses were so empty that ample accommodation was available for troops if necessary.

At first the sub-committees met, but one by one members withdrew until the business was left pretty much in the hands of the parish priest. The Protestant clergy soon found that their attendance was useless. The people to be relieved were almost exclusively Roman Catholic, and neither would it be expedient that Protestant clergy should visit their houses, nor could they well object to lists of

O

parishioners vouched for by the priests. Loud complaints were made by the unsuccessful, and the popularity of many a parish priest fell to zero. Instances were openly given of the number of people with money, meal, and cattle whose names were returned on the lists ; but, like the shooting of the obnoxious landlord who had two estates, what was everybody's business was nobody's business, and no representations were made on the subject. In some parishes the lists were returned by the person who collected the priest's dues. The priest said he knew best the people in want ; but disappointed parishioners complained that those only whose dues were paid appeared upon the list. On the days for distribution crowds assembled round every committee-room. Farmers' wives with plenty at home were not ashamed to beg for meal. "Ah! sure," one said apologetically, as she gossiped in the waiting crowd, "It will do for the cows, the cratures!" Tradesmen followed suit. The smith left his forge and the shoemaker his last. Men with hundreds in the bank got meal; gombeen men got it; shopkeepers got it; and the misdirection of charity reached its culminating point when a grant of meal was made to a man who kept a bacon and flour store.

All this time the knot of agitators assured the well-dressed people, who could afford to deck themselves in gorgeous regalia, that they were starving ; at the same time recommending them to join the

Land League and pay up their subscriptions ; that rent was a robbery and any action calculated to deter its exaction a virtue ; that while crying for food they asked for no charity, but demanded as a right the return of some of the money robbed from the people by the tyranny of landlords and the rapacity of an alien Government.

That these principles were adopted may explain the extraordinary want of self-respect with which people clamoured for relief. That they were adopted in their entirety is too unhappily shown in the return of agrarian offences committed between the 1st of May and 31st of January, in which period 977 agrarian offences were committed in Ireland, more than half that number being committed in Connaught. When it is remembered that these offences include such as killing of cattle or maiming them by cutting out their tongues and cutting off their tails, tearing out the tongues of horses, or smashing the legs of sheep, because rent has been paid or a farm taken, it will be seen with what ferocity the new agrarian gospel was propagated.

The funds were now in full work, and from every part of the world subscriptions came in. The English public began to suspect that there was more in the cry of famine than met the eye, and the English subscriptions were in consequence not one-third of the amount to which under other circumstances they would have amounted. Australia came nobly to the front, and America and Canada poured their thousands of dollars into the Irish fund. Yet the commissioners from American papers of repute could find no famine. The *New York Herald* and the *Chicago Tribune* sent men who saw with their own eyes, and reported that while there was distress in some parts of the west there was nothing approaching to a famine. The English papers were reticent, for a denial would look like a defence, and unfortunately they were almost committed to a famine by the Duchess of Marlborough's appeal. Among the Irish people the feeling grew that as money was being sent into the country it was no disgrace to get as much as one could.

"Yes, sir," said a blacksmith one day, "I am badly treated; every one in the street except myself is getting the meal, and I have as good a right to it as they have."

"Perhaps they are poorer than you, and you don't require it."

"Not at all, sir. Don't I see them going and selling it every morning down at Brady's shop?"

"Have you applied to the relieving-officer for relief?"

"Oh, Lord, no, sir! sure I don't want it that way; but when it's going, haven't I as good a right to get it as another?"

"Well," I said, "take my advice, and if you want to make a few shillings go and finish the gate I saw you working at this morning. You will be more happy afterwards than if you took this charity, and perhaps kept the meal from some one who required it."

He thought for a moment; then, saying, " Begorra, then, that's what I'll do, I'll work for it," he went away, content as a last resource to work for his daily bread.

In the far west the consignments of meal were not even secure until legally distributed. The people of Slyne Head came to the conclusion that in the distribution of the meal at Clifden undue favour was shown to other neighbourhoods, and, like the blacksmith, they were determined to "have their share of what was going." One fine day they boarded a hooker, becalmed off the head, with a consignment of meal on board for the Clifden Relief Committee. There was other meal on board, of which they took none, but they settled the matter of distribution to Slyne Head for a time by helping themselves to as much of the relief meal as they considered their due. Thus the distribution has gone on for five months, and now, when the time approaches when real pressure may be felt in many districts, the funds so lavishly expended have nearly reached their limit of supply.

Why, it may be asked, was no person found with sufficient public spirit to expose the exaggerated statements and misdirected charity in some localities? There are two reasons. As a rule the gentry have held aloof from the distribution of these relief funds, and left it almost entirely in the hands of the clergy. Had there been a real famine they would probably have been drawn to the aid of the people ; but the anti-rent agitation has for the present placed a terrible gap between landlord and tenant that only time will close. But even if one were found with moral and physical courage to expose the way in which the cry of famine was being used to accentuate the proposition of the Land League that landlordism in Ireland is the cause of recurring famines, in answer to his statements her Grace's appeal would be quoted, as if it referred to all Ireland. The mere suspicion, mentioned from a Western pulpit, that a member of the congregation had made statements calculated to prevent money being granted to the parish, sent the congregation *en masse* rushing to his pew. Had he not brought his revolver with him he would never have left the chapel alive.

Among the evils of the famine cry I do not class Major Nolan's Seeds Bill. Naturally every farmer tried to obtain new seed, even at the high price at which they were sold by the union. No doubt the feeling is universal that payment will never be demanded. Probably the disappearance of so much of the four millions of Irish Church Surplus would be regarded with equanimity by either party, and even if the money be not paid, the bestowal of new potato seed, in place of the old worn-out greentops, cannot be called an unproductive gift. Here the benefit of the Seeds

Bill ends. The boards of guardians contracted locally for oats. The contractors bought oats from the farmers, and, mixing the different kinds, sold the mixture to the guardians, who distributed it as new seed. As the different kinds of oats will come in at different times, the mixed crop will be a serious loss to those unfortunate enough to take the seed on the conditions laid down in the Act.

I do not mean to convey that there has been no distress in Ireland, or that great pressure may not be felt for the next two months. In certain districts there would have been distress necessitating an appeal to the poor rates but for the relief granted through the various funds. But one fact remains to show how hollow is the cry of famine. The average poor rate in the west of Ireland does not exceed 1s. 8d. in the pound, and in some unions in which large sums have been expended in charity the rates are one penny in the pound less than last year. That the farmers of Ireland could not have borne any increased rate is absurd. Thirty millions of Irish farmers' money lie on deposit in savings and other Irish banks, and bankers know well how much of this money is made up by the deposits of the small farmers. In round numbers £500,000 has been subscribed, besides the money borrowed by landlords and by sanitary authorities. Had the distress been met with the poor rate, one-sixth of this sum would have been sufficient. Loans could, if necessary, have been obtained by the unions for extraordinary expenditure (though in very few unions would the amount of increased expenditure have reached 1s. 6d. in the pound) ; and the spectacle would have been spared of a population, demoralized by free gifts, day after day neglecting their business with eleemosynary languor, and proclaiming by their presence at the lottery of the committee-rooms, "We will not dig ; to beg we are not ashamed."

III.

LOOKING back to the Duchess of Marlborough's letter of the 16th of December, the first appeal made on behalf of the Irish people, it might have been expected that out of the ready response given by England would have grown to a certain extent a feeling of gratitude in Irish breasts. Committees were quickly formed, and from that fund came the first assurance that no Irish cry of distress would pass unheeded. But it is a singular fact that among the people the name of the Duchess of Marlborough was seldom heard, the funds being generally alluded to as "American money." Those who recognized the fact that England had sub-scribed only did so to contrast the comparative smallness of her subscription with that of Australia, and statements were made that England would be only too glad to see her poorer sister perish. Besides, however disaffected a large section of the Irish people may be, they look upon it as England's duty to come to their assistance whenever they may call, and accept the aid demanded as a small instalment of their plundered property.

Even the members of the committees for the distribution of the Duchess of Marlborough's fund were not always unanimous in the acknowledgment of her Grace's benevolent intentions. At one of the committees where the parson and the priest worked amicably together, the former proposed a resolution conveying the thanks of the committee to the Duchess of Marlborough. The priest was asked to second it, but declined on the plea that "he was not in the habit of paying compliments to ladies." The fact is that from the first the Irish people either believed, or affected to believe, that the institution of the Duchess of Marlborough's fund was a bid for popularity, and the repeated suggestions from her Grace that money should be remitted for distribution to that fund rather than that of the Mansion House was quoted as a proof that her appeal had not been made exclusively from charitable motives. That this belief, or affected belief, was erroneous, there can be no doubt; but the fact remains that, so far as the English subscriptions are concerned, charity must be its own reward.

The distribution of private charity has always been a difficult problem; but when a nation descends to crave for alms, the evils of free distribution cannot be exaggerated. The moral weakness and loss of self-dependence that injures the recipient is intensified a thousandfold when a large section of a community has learned that improvidence has no Nemesis, and money or money's worth is to be had for the asking. Not that it may not be necessary in extreme circumstances to appeal for help to the world. But who ever heard of such an appeal except when home resources had broken down, or were manifestly insufficient to meet the crisis? The Irish demand has been as if a family, with thirty millions put by and an income of thirty millions a year, appealed for external help while the reserve fund was practically untouched, and without waiting for a strain upon the resources set apart for the support of the weaker members. No doubt the income was sensibly diminished and the number to be supported sensibly increased, but the distress would have been amply provided for by an expenditure of £300,000, if levied off the rates; and that Ireland should have posed before the world as a mendicant for an amount that would not have represented sixpence in the pound on its income is destructive to its self-respect as it is humiliating to every honest Irishman.

I quote £300,000, about one-half of the sum distributed, for few in Ireland deny that more than half the funds have been wasted. The probable effect of meeting the distress through the rates was shown in a Western union, where a Local Govern-

ment inspector, struck with the apparent poverty
of a number of the inhabitants of a certain district,
ordered that they should be supplied with outdoor
relief. The consequence was that the ratepayers of
the district waited upon the board of guardians
and protested against an expenditure which they
knew to be unnecessary. How many hundreds of
pounds from the relief funds might not have been
spent in the district without protest! It must not
be imagined that those who objected were hard-
hearted, or prepared to leave their poor neighbours
to die rather than permit any increase to their poor
rate. The bad qualities of Irishmen of that class
(for which England has in the past been largely
responsible) are exposed often enough ; but among
them cannot be counted the callousness that would
see a neighbour in want without coming to his
succour. To their honour be it said that in such a
case their private charity would not be appealed to
in vain.

The action, then, of the ratepayers in that district was full of significance. With the assurance
of famine, it was declared that what the people
wanted was work, not alms ; but when work was
provided it was not always found that such an
independent spirit asserted itself. The effect of
the distribution of meal was that in some instances
the men for whose benefit loans had been applied
for by the landlords refused to execute the work,
except on payment of double the rate of wages

then ruling in the neighbourhood.   The works were of course abandoned, and the money granted by the Board of Works remains in their hands.

It is asserted that the people most affected by the distress are the small ratepaying farmers, and under the poor law they could not obtain relief without first relinquishing their little farms.   It is true that many small farmers have felt the distress severely, and under the poor law could not have been afforded relief; but the Government has since determined that relief is to be given, if necessary, to ratepayers of over £4 valuation.   As to those rated under that amount, such an order could have been issued six months ago if necessary.   In the event of the poor rate pressing unduly, loans could have been granted then as now to the unions, and the persons relieved might have received without shame a portion of the fund to which they had themselves contributed, and to whose aid they were legally entitled.

But such a course would not have suited the views of the unscrupulous section that has made political capital out of an Irish famine.   To bring the land laws before the world it was necessary that something startling must take place.   What more startling than a famine?   And what so great a proof that the land laws must be at fault?   So we have had the famine, fortunately without its horrors.   And, the ground being thus prepared, the first seedling of the new crop of proposed legislation has been planted by Mr. O'Connor Power, in the shape of his short bill enabling a man evicted for non-payment of rent to claim an amount equal to seven years' rent for disturbance. By this measure I can take a farm at £20 a year, and, having paid no rent for three years, on being evicted I can claim £140 for disturbance, and take my chance of what the county-court judge may allow for unexhausted manures.

Since the inauguration of the anti-rent agitation the Irish landlords have been execrated from a hundred platforms on both sides of the Atlantic. To their rapacity was attributed the primary cause of the famine, and it was declared that in their greed they squeezed the last penny from their hunger-stricken tenants. It may be well, then, to inquire what the landlords have done to assist the people ; and it must not be forgotten that the anti-rent movement was avowedly for the purpose of depreciating property and forcing estates into the market, that Government might purchase at a low figure and resell to the tenants.

Mr. Parnell calculated that the remission of rents made by the landlords would reach the enormous figure of four millions; but, allowing 50 per cent. for his enthusiasm, it is certain that very nearly half that amount has been remitted to the tenants, and that while the landlords were being reviled as the destroyers of the people, they were themselves feeling the pinch of poverty more bitterly than the people by whom the abatement was demanded. Add to the two millions £1,250,000 granted as loans, by which employment could be given on their properties, and we find that the much-abused landlords have given towards the Irish "famine" more than six times the entire amount of the subscriptions from all parts of the world.

Knowing what we now know of this battle without slain, the expediency of the inauguration of a great subscription, in accordance with the extravagant statements made from the anti-rent platforms, would appear to be questionable. If, without a death from starvation or a strain upon the poor rates, over three millions can be secured in hard cash by an inexpensive agitation, there are few ventures in political warfare that offer results so substantial as the producing of a famine to order.

THE END.

PRINTED BY WILLIAM CLOWES AND SONS, LIMITED, LONDON AND BECCLES.